SPECIAL FOREWORD

At USAllianz Investor Services, LLC® (USAllianz®) we believe in four fundamental values that should underlie all sincere efforts to help people retire. First, someone has to take the time to educate consumers about what they're facing and what they can do about it. Second, people need access to financial professionals who really know how to plan for retirement—because it's much different than planning for any other stage of life. Third, we need new products and new services that respond to the unique challenges of managing money during retirement. And finally, today's retirees have to be able to count on the knowledge and integrity of their financial professionals and the financial strength of the companies standing behind the products they rely on.

I hope this book finds its way to the top of everyone's reading list—because it provides a lot of the education we need. I think it will change the way people look at retirement planning while giving them a much better understanding of what they can do to help themselves. I also think it will enhance the conversations people are having with their financial professionals. Getting a handle on the complexities of retirement planning isn't always easy, but it's much more difficult if you don't have a grasp of the fundamentals. People need a big-picture understanding and a clear framework to take action. This book provides both.

USAllianz® has always been committed to developing the kinds of products and services people need to address their financial concerns, and now more than ever we are focused on retirement. Our new variable products provide innovative options to the all important issues of accumulating enough assets, providing a stream of income, and offering protection for your beneficiaries. As a division of Allianz Life Insurance Company of North America, we know that the benefits and guarantees we offer are only as good as our own company, so we strive to live up to the highest standards.

It's a pleasure for me to be able to write a foreword to Paul's book. He and his company are truly committed to helping people manage their money better during retirement, and so are we. We've taught thousands of financial professionals how to "invest right during retirement," and continue to help them get this important message out to their clients. We've worked hard in the last few years to educate financial professionals and consumers while developing a lineup of new products that take retirement planning to a whole new level. This book will help us do an even better job.

If you ultimately find yourself looking for a financial professional who can help you with everything Paul talks about in this book, feel free to give us a call—we know a lot of them. And when it's time to implement your plan, please don't hesitate to ask your financial professionals about our products. They were designed with The Grangaard Strategy™ in mind.

Christopher H. Pinkerton
President and CEO
USAllianz Investor Services, LLC®
1-800-542-5427

The
GRANGAARD
STRATEGY™

Invest Right During Retirement

PAUL GRANGAARD, CPA

A Perigee Book

A Perigee Book
Published by The Berkley Publishing Group
A division of Penguin Putnam Inc.
375 Hudson Street
New York, New York 10014

Special sales edition: January 2003
Not for resale.

Perigee special sales edition ISBN: 0-399-52926-8

Visit our website at www.penguinputnam.com

Printed in the United States of America

10 9 8 7 6 5 4 3 2 1

For Max, David, and Carol

*This book could never have been written without the love
and support of my sons and my wife—Max and David for having the
incredible patience to let me write it, and Carol for doing
literally everything else.*

DISCLAIMERS

The ideas presented in this book are based upon the application of a particular methodology of managing investments for retirement planning. Other models for investing exist in the investment world and some of these may be more suitable for some people under certain circumstances. The methodology presented in this book is for analyzing individual situations and is not a guarantee of any particular investment strategy or result. Readers assume full responsibility for deciding whether the ideas in this book will help them achieve their desired results and for selecting all investments and investment strategies used in their own financial plans.

This publication is designed to provide accurate and authoritative information in regard to the subject matter covered. It is published with the understanding that the publisher and author are not engaged in rendering legal, financial, accounting, or other professional services. If legal, financial, accounting, or other professional advice is required the services of a competent professional should be sought.

The information provided in this book is for general and informational purposes only and should not be considered an individualized recommendation or personalized investment advice. Although all reasonable efforts have been made to ensure that the information contained in this book is accurate as of the date of publication, the author and the publisher disclaim any liability with respect to the accuracy or timeliness of the information.

Before you go any further there are a few important points you need to be aware of. First, the investment performance data we will be using is historical and does not reflect sales or investment management charges. Second, you should always remember that past performance is not indicative of future results. We often use it to gain a sense of the reasonableness of our own assumptions, but there can never be any guarantee that the past will be able to predict the future. Third, as an investor, your investment returns and the value of your principal will fluctuate, so when redeemed, your shares may be worth more or less than original cost. Investment shares are always subject to investment risk, including the possible loss of principal invested. And finally, the equity, or stock market investments we will be talking about in this book are not insured by the FDIC and are not deposits or other obligations of, or guaranteed by, any depository institution.

All financial organizations and software publishers include a disclaimer that tells users that there is no warranty that their method is correct, and that the work is presented "AS IS." I would like to caution you to read the disclaimer in the front of this book that says that we also present this material "AS IS" and make no warranties—implied or otherwise.

CONTENTS

PART ONE

New Realities

Understanding the major periods and phases of retirement •
An overview of managing your money during retirement •
Outdated approaches that don't work • Minimum required
distribution rules and the "liquidity tax"

The dramatic increases in life expectancy • The consequences of living longer

Planning for inflation-adjusted income • Dealing with fluctuating income needs during retirement • Budgeting for the
"right amount" of retirement income • Understanding the
difference between purchasing power and income

PART TWO

Managing Your Retirement Resources

Creating dependable income for the rest of your life •
Sources of income in retirement • Building Income Ladders •
Understanding fixed-income investments: learning about
bonds • Managing Income Ladders during retirement •
Using annuities for income

PART THREE
Flexibility, Comfort, and Control

The different segments of the stock market • The importance of diversification during retirement • How stock market performance changes from year to year • Deciding which stocks to sell

Try not to pay "liquidity taxes" in retirement • The value of investing in tax-deferred accounts • The consequences of investing in taxable accounts • Rethinking annuities • Different ways you can be taxed in retirement

Applying the Grangaard Strategy™ • Testing your portfolio with shorter holding periods • Creating "deferred" Income Ladders • The consequences of investing too conservatively

The assumptions and variables that go into a smart retirement plan • Figuring out how much capital you need to get the income you want • Using the worksheets and look-up tables • Figuring out how much income you can get from the assets you already have • Getting some help

ACKNOWLEDGMENTS

How do you acknowledge all the people who contribute to the creation of a book or the development of an idea? In my case, there have been many important people along the way who helped provide the intellectual foundation upon which the Grangaard Strategy™ is built. Of course it's not just the direct influences that count. The financial world is an ocean of concepts and ideas that have been developed and refined by hundreds of people over thousands of years. We are all the beneficiaries of that history of creativity and hard work.

The toughest job for me has been to figure out how to tell this story in a way that nonfinancial people will understand. It wouldn't have been possible to do that without the commitment of John Duff, my editor at Perigee. John has never been willing to let this project be less than he knew it could be, and the result is a book that is much better than it ever could have been without him. Of course I would never have met John had it not been for the vision and diligence of my agent, Ken Atchity. While producing two movies and working on a number of other projects he still found the time and energy to find a home for this book.

I also owe a special debt of gratitude to my friends and business associates at Financial Education, Inc. Larry Atkins and I have traveled around the country teaching the professional community how to manage money during retirement. His efforts in polishing our message and teaching it to others have helped us impact thousands of financial advisors—and through them, even more of their clients.

Roger Katzenmaier has helped me understand much about retirement investing, and his son Kevin did a lot of marvelous work on our original corporate website. Their contributions have been greatly appreciated.

And finally, thank you to David Reitan for keeping the faith all these years and helping out in the back office. We would never have made it without your generosity and support.

FOREWORD

Many years ago when I was a young boy on the farm my grand-father told me that the secret to happiness as we grow older is learning how to live our lives rather than living out our lives. As a financial planner for more than thirty-five years I realize the power of those words more than ever.

My experience has taught me that the difference between being old and being elderly is often the amount of monthly income we have. As a result, I have focused my practice on help-ing clients understand that in retirement real wealth is measured by sustainable income.

With three master's degrees and six financial designations I thought I was familiar with the correct planning concepts to help my clients determine how much wealth they needed to accumulate to provide their retirement income. But my life and practice changed forever on Saturday, April 15, 1998, when I was invited to attend a financial planning workshop for retirees in Saint Paul, Minnesota. The seminar was conducted by Paul Grangaard, and I left realizing that I had been doing it all wrong. I was disillusioned and angry with my profession because after all the formal education, no book, no speaker, and no seminar had ever discussed what I heard from Paul.

Driving back to Fargo that evening I remember being plagued by a single thought—"If my retired clients don't know how to manage their money during retirement, how do they know if they have accumulated enough?" It hit me like a ton of bricks. The right way to do it was the opposite of what I had been taught as a professional for thirty-five years. All of my software and all of my training had told me to set retirement accumulation targets based upon time, return, and deposits before retirement, and then assume a straight-line withdrawal for income during retirement—which is the opposite of what my clients need to do in retirement. This revelation changed my life and my practice forever.

Paul Grangaard teaches profound concepts to help retirees live their lives rather than living out their lives. These ideas will become a paradigm for future retirees—because the question in retirement is not whether to have growth or income, but to have both growth and income. Retirees don't go to the pharmacy with their financial statements; they go with their checkbooks.

The Grangaard Strategy™ is a launching pad for retirees and financial professionals. Once read and practiced it will provide new ways of living our lives with less of the economic despera-tion felt by so many seniors.

I have two sons, Brent and Corey, and grandchildren as well, who will someday be discussing retirement issues with their financial planners. I am confident this book will be part of how they manage their own money during retirement.

Thank you, Paul, for helping reduce economic suffering in the lives of so many retirees.

Larry Atkins, CFP®, CLU, MSFS, ChFC, CSA

PREFACE

Can you afford to retire and still maintain a reasonable lifestyle? Do you know how much money you need to do that next year, or in two years, or in ten? Do you know when you can stop working? Most people don't. The fact is, you can't even begin to answer these questions until you know how to manage your money during retirement. After all, how can you know how much to accumulate for retirement if you don't know how to manage it during retirement?

I have been teaching financial professionals and individuals how to manage money during retirement for a long time. In the past few years I focused primarily on professionals because I felt that by helping more of them I could also help more of you. I have been providing professional education courses for CPAs, attorneys, financial planners, and insurance agents around the country and have been working with some of the biggest financial services organizations in the world.

But the time has come to take this important message directly to you, the financial consumer. Millions of people will be retiring in the next ten to fifteen years and many of them haven't spent any time at all thinking about how to manage their financial resources during the "spending" phase of life. There's an old proverb that says, "it's not what you know that will hurt you, and it's not what you know you don't know that will hurt you—it's what you don't know you don't know that will get you into trouble." There are a lot of things you probably don't know you don't know about managing money during retirement. It's time to change that!

Understanding how to invest during retirement was not such a big deal in the past when most people lived on pensions and social security. Today, not only will you be living longer in retirement, but you will also be managing more and more of your own money. Traditional company-managed pension plans are becoming a thing of the past. Social security is questionable and many people have a lot of their money in self-administered 401(k) plans and IRAs. This is a state of affairs that my friend and colleague Roger Katzenmaier compares to hiring untrained air-traffic controllers off the street—we are just bound to have a lot of casualties. This book should help you do a better job facing these new realities in retirement.

Many people ask me if this is a do-it-yourself manual for retirement planning—in some ways it is, and in some ways it isn't. *The Grangaard Strategy*™ is dedicated to the proposition that you can understand what you need to know about this important topic—but it doesn't necessarily follow that you can do it all yourself. In fact, there is never a more important time to work with a qualified financial professional. There are just too many aspects to financial management in retirement to try to go it alone.

Although it certainly makes sense to get some help, you still have to know what you're doing—at least in general terms. You need to be able to talk intelligently with your advisors and you need to be able to determine whether they know what they're talking about and whether their approach and your approach are in sync. Selecting a financial professional is one of the most important decisions you will ever make, and the information in this book should help you make a better choice.

I have said for years in my financial planning workshops that the ultimate goal of effective retirement planning is to help people sleep better at night and live better during the day. In other words, you need to manage your money during retirement in a way that provides the income you need and the lifestyle you want without having to take so many investment risks that you can't sleep at night.

I also tell retirees that one of the biggest risks they face today is not losing their money in the stock market—but outliving it! People have to learn how to protect their assets while also putting them to work to provide the lifestyle they need and want.

At my company, Financial Education, Inc. we are dedicated to the idea that everyone can learn how to manage money during retirement. We are also committed to providing the tools and training professionals need to help their clients in these areas. We offer a wide range of seminars, books, tapes, CDs, software programs, and other materials to do that. In addition, we provide employee education seminars for major corporations across the country.

So read this book. You will understand it, because it isn't that complicated. I believe it will change the way you think about investing for the rest of your life.

Paul A. Grangaard, CPA
Saint Paul, Minnesota

The
GRANGAARD
STRATEGY™

The Twelve Principles of Twenty-First-Century Retirement Investing

Traditional financial planning theory says that to figure out how much income you can get from your retirement assets all you have to do is assume an interest rate and a life expectancy, plug everything into a calculator, push a few buttons, and see how much you can get before you run out. Wrong! This is not the way to do it!

First of all, it's not just an interest rate you have to assume, it's a total rate of return. Second, you can't really plan exactly when you'll run out of money because you don't know when you're going to die. Third, there is a big difference between earning a rate of return and being able to use it for income. In retirement, things are not exactly what they seem—or what they were before you retired.

So what are you supposed to do? Unfortunately, most people

revert to old rules of thumb. They either put their money into conservative investments, live as frugally as they can, and hope they don't run out too soon, or they use some kind of one-size-fits-all asset allocation strategy to figure out how much to put into the stock market—usually based upon their age and some fuzzy notion of their "risk tolerance."

Today's and tomorrow's retirees need to know a lot more than that about managing money during retirement. You need better information, you need better advice, and you need it now! You need to be smarter consumers, you need new ideas that fit new realities, and you need more science and less psychology. You need real, honest, serious help and many people haven't been getting it. It takes more than a few anecdotes, some old clichés, and a bunch of outdated guidelines to teach you how to manage a portfolio to maintain safe, steady, dependable income for thirty- or forty-year retirement periods—and that's exactly what most of us have to do. Managing money during retirement requires an "income-first" investment approach that few advisors and even fewer consumers may know anything about.

Today, we are all being forced to become our own pension-plan managers. Unfortunately, most of us don't have MBAs in finance and investing and we haven't been given the training we need to do it right. This book uses the Twelve Principles of Twenty-First-Century Retirement Investing to show you what to do and how to do it. Consider it a mini-MBA in retirement finance. It takes you far beyond the pop psychology and razzmatazz of glitzy new investment trends. It takes you straight to the issues and shows you step-by-step what to do about them. Most people don't realize that managing money during retirement, while they're spending it, is completely different than managing money before retirement, while they're accumulating it. I'll show you why, and I'll show you what to do about it.

The concepts and ideas in this book should help you gain the financial flexibility, comfort, and control you're looking for—whether you have ten thousand dollars or one million dollars, and whether you're retiring today or twenty years from now. If you're already retired, if you're sixty-five and getting ready to take the plunge, or even if you're forty-five and trying to figure out how much more you need to save, this book is for you!

The Real World: Snapshot #1

One of the biggest risks many elderly investors face today is the risk of outliving their money. It's not just the risk of fluctuating stock prices or the default risk on bonds. One of the worst things they face is the risk of running out of money too soon, and a big part of an advisor's job is to help them understand this risk and show them what to do about it.

People are living a lot longer and it's putting a great deal of pressure on their retirement assets. Some seventy-year-olds are still looking after their ninety-five-year-old parents! Believe me, they know exactly what I mean about running out of money too soon—because they're seeing it happen to people they love.

Marc C. Hadley, CFP®, Manager of Personal Financial Planning, Wilkerson, Guthmann + Johnson, Ltd., Saint Paul, Minnesota

The Real World: Snapshot #2

My associate, Larry Atkins, and I were traveling together recently to present a retirement planning seminar to a group of financial professionals. On the way to the conference we were swapping stories about friends and relatives we know in retirement, and about what's happening with their investment portfolios. Many of the stories went something like this.

A friend, we'll call him Bob, stops by after playing a round of golf with three of his buddies. He tells you that it was one of the most depressing afternoons of his life. Since it has been a cold spring and is one of the nicest days of early summer, you remark that you're surprised he didn't enjoy himself—even if he hadn't played well. "Oh, I played fine, and the weather was great," says Bob, "that's not it at all. The problem," he continues, "is that my friends are so depressed about the stock market and what's going on with their investments that we couldn't enjoy the golf. Interest rates are so low that one of the guys, who's probably the most financially conservative of the bunch, can't stop talking about how much less he's earning, how badly his lifestyle is suffering, and how hard he's working to find some higher yields. The other guys, who are both much more aggressive investors, have really gotten burned in the stock market lately. They can't stop fretting about which stocks to sell—at big losses, to get the money they need to pay the bills or go out for a bite to eat. These guys are over-invested in the stock market and they are really suffering because of it."

Bob also tells you that he is having a hard time letting his friends in on the investment strategy he and his financial advisor implemented a few years ago because he doesn't want them to get any more depressed than they already are. He says that he has investments set aside to take care of his income for many years, and that the rest of his money is invested to go after the growth he needs to maintain that income for the rest of his life.

He then says that he feels like he's in pretty good shape right now. He knows he won't need more income for a long time and he knows he won't be forced to sell stock market investments any time soon. In other words, he doesn't seem to be losing any sleep over recent market conditions. So while his buddies are out chasing interest rates, selling stocks at a loss, and cutting back on their lifestyles, he and his wife are doing exactly what they want to do, when they want to do it—because they worked with a qualified financial professional to create a smart retirement plan in the first place.

We probably all know people in circumstances similar to Bob and his friends—and some of them are in better financial shape than others.

The Real World: Snapshot #3

My father is a retired college professor. He and my mother enjoy a healthy and active retirement. All my grandparents lived well into their nineties—so both my mother and father can boast about the longevity in their families. But they know they have to plan for a long retirement.

The state of the stock market affects them, but not nearly as much as some other people who have most of their money in self-managed retirement accounts like IRAs, annuities, and mutual funds. As a retired college professor my dad has a state-sponsored pension plan that pays him a substantial monthly income for the rest of his life—and it's even adjusted for inflation. If he dies my mother continues to get it. With the pension and Social Security my mom and dad can live just fine. So you might wonder: Is the Grangaard Strategy™ important for the Grangaards? The answer is yes.

My father was a diligent saver throughout his life. By the time he got to retirement a few years ago he had accumulated a fair amount of money in the tax-sheltered savings plans to which he had access as a college professor. He and my mother don't really "need" the income they get from these investments, but they sure enjoy it. My dad calls it his "fun money" and my mom likes the freedom it gives her to be less concerned about a budget.

However, in addition to the extra income these assets provide, my parents also see this money as a big part of their legacy. The Social Security and monthly pension payments stop when they die, so except for their house and personal property there wouldn't be much left to pass on to their kids and grandkids. They see these other assets as a way to enhance what they will ultimately be able to do for all of us. So they have two goals in mind. They want to maintain a legacy for their family and they want to get as much income as they can for themselves.

The Real World: A Summary

Everyone comes to retirement in unique circumstances and with a different bag of "financial cats and dogs." Some people have the majority of their assets in 401(k) plans or rollover IRAs. Some, like my mom and dad, are set up pretty well with pension plans. Others may be selling a home or business or be planning to live off rents or royalties or the value of alternative assets like real estate. And of course most of us will get something from Social Security. But it's different for everyone—so you have to sort out the specifics of your own situation and deal with them on an individual, case-by-case basis. As you will see, the Twelve Principles of Twenty-First-Century Retirement Investing are applicable to you no matter what your current circumstances and regardless of how your assets are currently invested.

Principle #1: Expect to Outlive the Averages

Never before have so many people retired so early, lived so long, and been so completely on their own. The aging of America and the accelerated growth in self-managed retirement accounts like 401(k) plans and rollover IRAs has set the stage for a national financial crisis.

The research is clear. The growing population of older Americans has to make its money last a lot longer. According to *65+ in the United States,* a study by the U.S. Bureau of the Census, the "old-old," those over the age of eighty-five, are the fastest-growing segment of the population, and "recent improvements in the chances of survival at the end of the age spectrum have emerged as the most important factor in the growth of the oldest old." The report goes on to say that "the average expectation of additional years of life at age 65 has increased by 46 percent between 1900 and 1991." In fact, it shows that the number of sixty-five-year-olds in 1940 who lived to be at least ninety years old was only 7 percent. By 1960 it had doubled to 14 percent. It just about doubled again to 26 percent by 2000, and it is expected to increase to 42 percent by 2050.

Don't Plan to Run Out of Money Too Soon

Current life-expectancy tables indicate that the average life expectancy of a sixty-five-year-old today is about twenty years.

In other words, at age sixty-five today, you can plan on average to live to about age eighty-five. But that's only an average. And averages are just averages. They don't relate to you, or to me, or to anyone else. The fact is, very few of us will actually live to an average age of eighty-five. About half of us won't live that long, while the other half will live longer—and some of us a lot longer. The problem is that none of us know which half we're in. And because we don't, we all have to plan to live longer than average, because we know at least half of us will. In fact, if we don't all plan to live longer than average, almost half of us may be planning to run out of money too soon!

Unfortunately, the fact that we are living longer also leads to other serious planning concerns—like inflation and fluctuating lifestyles.

Principle #2: Adjust for Changing Income Needs

Although inflation wasn't such a big problem when people didn't live as long, it's a critical issue today. Increasing life expectancies force all of us to be much more concerned about inflation. Even at the lower rates of the last few years you have to be prepared to double your income over a typical thirty-year retirement period—just to maintain your lifestyle. At higher rates you'll need to do a lot more than that.

You also have to be able to anticipate your long-term retirement income needs—and it's not quite as simple as taking a percentage of your preretirement income and adjusting it for inflation every year. Like most people, you will probably run into circumstances in which you need more money in some years and less in others. You have to take these fluctuations into account when doing your planning.

Principle #3: Create Dependable Income for the Rest of Your Life

Essentially, at retirement, you want to put yourself back into the same financial position you were in before you retired. While you were working, you got your income, or as financial planners would say, your liquidity, from your wages. As a result, you were probably more comfortable investing some of your retirement savings in the stock market for the higher rates of return they have provided over the years. You knew you wouldn't be forced to sell them anytime soon to get the income you needed to support yourself and your family because you got a paycheck every couple weeks—so you were able to be a long-term investor on the stock market side of your portfolio.

However, when you retire, you have to get both your growth and income from your retirement assets—which is a much different ball game. Managing a rollover IRA to provide safe, steady, dependable income is a lot more difficult than going to the bank to cash a paycheck. But that's the challenge you face. You have to manage your money during retirement to go after the growth you may need in the stock market while also being able to replace the paycheck you no longer have.

In the story about Bob and his golfing buddies two things are clear. First, Bob's friends' problems are directly related to their need for income, and second, Bob's comfort is directly related to the fact that his income needs have already been taken care of. Bob's conservative friend is worried because his interest income has taken a dive, and his aggressive friends are concerned because they are being forced to sell stocks at a loss to get the money they need to live on. Bob, however, still has seven or eight years of dependable income set aside because he purchased the appropriate amount of fixed-income investments a few years ago—which is just one of the ways you can create your own Income Ladders.

Use Income Ladders to Replace Your Paycheck

Creating Income Ladders is a key element in replacing your paycheck during retirement while also protecting yourself against some of the problems your ultraconservative friends may be running into. Income Ladders can be constructed in many ways— but they almost always use fixed-income investments to provide the income and liquidity you lose when you stop working. You can use a variety of different investments such as single-premium immediate annuities, bonds or CDs—but whatever products or investments work best in your own circumstances, Income Ladders are a tool you can use to provide the safe, steady, dependable income you need to replace your paychecks in retirement. Income Ladders will probably be a vital part of your retirement.

Don't Let Your Lifestyle Slip Away

Luckily, the fact that we are living so much longer can be part of the solution to many of our investment problems in retirement—because it allows us to take advantage of the power of compounding, or earning interest on the interest. Unfortunately, most people don't know how important compounding is during retirement, which brings us to the next principle of twenty-first-century retirement investing.

Principle #4: Count on Compounding During Retirement

Longer retirement periods can mean longer compounding periods, and longer compounding periods can allow you to earn more interest on interest, or returns on returns, during retirement. Most of the income you generate and spend throughout retirement will probably come from the compounded returns on your retirement assets—not from the assets themselves. In fact, because of the power of compounding, you are likely to maintain the overall value of your investments while also generating larger amounts of income.

The Classic Dilemma: Liquidity versus Growth

Managing money during retirement brings into focus a classic investment dilemma. Generally, it can be distilled into a question of "liquidity" versus "growth." In most cases we want to have maximum access to our money (more liquidity), with the greatest opportunity for gain (more growth), and the smallest possible chance of loss (less risk).

The problem is that these objectives can be contradictory. Our need for liquidity and safety will often lead us to put our money into lower-return investments that may not provide the growth we need. On the other hand, an obsessive concern for growth may cause us to invest too aggressively in stock market investments that fluctuate more in value, carry higher levels of risk, and provide less access to our money. During retirement, we have to find the "sweet spot" that balances our need for liquidity with our need for growth—what I call "threading the financial needle."

Principle #5: Invest in the Right Stuff

You can't really appreciate the power of compounding until you see it working at different rates of investment return, and you also need to have a feel for which markets to invest in to have a chance of achieving these different rates of return. Most people don't understand the difference between compounding a historical fixed-income rate of return of 6 percent and a historical growth stock rate of return of 12 percent. The impact on accumulated values and retirement lifestyles can be amazing.

Being Too Aggressive or Too Conservative Can Cost You Big Bucks

Many people may need to invest some of their retirement assets in the stock market to have a shot at the higher rates of return they have historically provided. It may be the only way they can hope to accumulate enough money to maintain a reasonable inflation-adjusted lifestyle throughout a long retirement. But you probably don't want to be like Bob's overly aggressive golfing buddies who have so much invested in the stock market that there's nothing left over for safer, income-producing investments.

You probably also don't want to be like Bob's overly conservative friend and put all of your money into safer, lower-return assets. This is one of the most common mistakes people make. At retirement, most of us are inclined to want to protect our financial assets—as we should! After all, we need to make them last a long time. Unfortunately, this sense of urgency to protect our assets may often cause us to invest too conservatively. Protecting your retirement assets is a good idea, but it has to be viewed within the broader context of protecting your overall retirement lifestyle—which often may require you to own some investments with the potential to deliver higher rates of return. An overly narrow focus on asset protection alone can leave you vulnerable to a serious and perhaps even catastrophic erosion of your income and lifestyle.

Principle #6: Be a Long-Term Investor During Retirement

You may be able to address many of your financial challenges during retirement by maintaining a longer-term investment perspective. Having the time you need to make better investment decisions can have a dramatic effect on your ability to achieve your goals and objectives and may even keep you from having to invest too conservatively.

To understand why, you need to be familiar with one of the most important investment concepts of all—compound average annual returns. You probably run into them all the time in newspapers, advertisements, and financial magazines, but few people really know what they are. When used properly, they're one of the most important tools you have for managing your investments during retirement.

Compound average annual returns are simply the average rates of return that investments earn over periods of time greater than one year when earnings are reinvested—and they are very helpful in evaluating the long-term performance of assets that fluctuate in value. For example, earning a 7 percent rate of return in the first year, followed by a 35 percent rate of return in the second year and a loss of 20 percent in the third year is almost exactly the same as earning an average annual return of 5 percent per year in each of the three years. You can compute a compound average annual rate of return for any kind of investment that goes up and down in value like the stock market.

Understanding this concept is critical to being able to evaluate, compare, and manage your investments—especially during retirement.

Selling Stocks During Retirement

During retirement many of us are going to be overall sellers of stock market investments. As a result, you have to be very careful about deciding when to sell because you don't want to undo what the magic of compounding might already have accomplished for you. Being forced to sell stocks at the wrong time is one of the big problems you face in retirement, and what to do about it leads us to Principle #7.

Principle #7: Know When to Sell

If you're going to invest some of your money in the stock market during retirement you don't ever want to be in the position of Bob's more aggressive golfing buddies. You never want to be forced to sell stocks when markets are down. Just like before you retire, your stock market investments can help you get the growth you need to maintain your lifestyle during retirement, but you can only take advantage of that growth by periodically selling the stocks—and you never want to be forced to do that at the wrong time.

Try Not to Sell Stocks at the Wrong Time

The real problem with owning stocks during retirement is not that they will fluctuate in value—we know they will do that. The problem with owning stocks during retirement is that you may be forced to sell them to get the income you need to live on when markets are down—in which case you might be forced to lose money to get money because you may have to sell at a loss. You can reduce the possibility that you will ever have to do that by increasing the amount of time you have available to leave your money invested in the stock market. This is called "increasing your stock market holding periods."

Holding periods give you a measure of how much time you have to decide when to sell. They tell you how long you can stay invested to ride out the inevitable ups and downs. Holding periods are important in retirement investing because they can help you reduce the possibility of losing money in the stock market while increasing your chances of getting the reasonable rates of return you expect. It's a simple concept, but it's one of the centerpieces of effective retirement investing.

Principle #8: Don't Let Dollar-Price-Erosion Catch You Off-Guard

By giving you the time you need to make better decisions about when to sell stocks, holding periods can also protect you against dollar-price-erosion. Dollar-price-erosion takes place when you sell more shares of stock when the market is down and fewer shares when the market is up to provide the same amount of income throughout retirement. This is the opposite of what you should do, and it can happen frequently if your holding periods are not long enough to protect you from having to sell stocks too often.

You need to make good decisions about when to sell stocks, and you also need to make good decisions about which stocks to sell. The next principle of twenty-first-century retirement investing addresses the importance of maintaining a well-diversified stock portfolio during retirement, which may increase the odds that you will have something in a good position to sell when you need to.

Principle #9: Diversify

The goal of stock market diversification during retirement is a little different than before retirement, because you need to focus your attention on selling stocks. Essentially, you should allocate your money to enough different stock market investments to increase the chances that there will be something in a good position to sell whenever you need to get more income. Having a diversified portfolio of stock market investments with reasonable-length holding periods can help you do that. You will not only have more time to decide when to sell, but you may also have more options when it comes to deciding what to sell—and that's a powerful combination. You always have to remember that as important as diversification is in potentially reducing risk, it does not assure a profit and does not necessarily protect you against a loss in declining markets—but it can certainly help.

Principle #10: Keep It Tax Deferred

Reducing income taxes is an important part of any investment strategy, and it's particularly important in retirement. Since you will probably be selling stock market investments to get income during retirement, you want to be very careful about how you structure your portfolio to reduce the taxes you have to pay each time you sell stocks. There are many ways to protect yourself against what I call the "liquidity tax" and many types of investment products that can help.

Principle #11: Have a Plan

What most people really want in retirement is flexibility, comfort, and control. You know things are inevitably going to be different than you planned, so you need to maintain the flexibility necessary to adjust to changing circumstances. You also want the comfort of going to bed every night with the confidence that you can live the way you want to without worrying about whether you are spending too much or too little, as well as the control that only comes with a thorough understanding of how to manage your money during retirement.

The biggest fear most people have in retirement is the fear that they will spend too much too soon and ultimately run out of money. The second biggest fear people have in retirement is the fear that the fear of spending too much will keep them from spending as much as they could. What we all need to do in retirement is spend the "right amount," which means that we need to figure out what the "right amount" is—and you can't do that without a plan.

The Process Is Not That Complicated

Over a working lifetime you accumulate retirement assets in a variety of accounts—retirement plans, regular and Roth IRAs, annuities, taxable accounts, and so on. Then, as you draw closer to retirement, you have to start repositioning your assets to facilitate the "spending" phase of life.

Ultimately, this repositioning entails carving off an initial Income Ladder to provide the income you will need throughout your first stock market holding period. Having created many years worth of safe, steady, dependable income with your first Income Ladder, you should be able to leave the rest of your assets in the stock market without the fear of having to sell them too soon. As you spend the first Income Ladder, your stock market investments are designed to grow at the higher rates of return they have historically provided and are planned to ultimately replace the value of the first Income Ladder. After the first Income Ladder has been spent, some of the assets accumulating in the stock market can be sold to create another Income Ladder to provide the income you need throughout the next holding period. Again, the remaining stock market investments are designed to continue growing at higher rates of return and are planned to be available to create future Income Ladders. By using this approach you are likely to end up with a fair amount of money at the end of your life.

Work with a Financial Professional

You may have the time and inclination to do all of this yourself—and that's great! But many people will want to work with a financial professional. If there is ever a good time to use an expert it's during retirement. There are income tax and estate planning issues, retirement plan rules and regulations, and a variety of other complexities to deal with—in addition to the overall problem of managing your money. A financial professional should be able to help you in all of these areas.

But don't make the mistake of thinking you can leave everything to the experts. You need to understand the essentials of investing during retirement yourself in order to select the right team of advisors in the first place and to take your place as an integral part of that team. After all, it's your money and it's your life!

Principle #12: Take Action Now

Later in the book we provide some easy-to-use worksheets and look-up tables that will help you take your first step in applying the Grangaard Strategy™. They will help you consider many of the important variables and assumptions that go into crafting a smart retirement plan and help you get to work now! Remember—it's never too early and it's never too late to do your financial planning.

Finding a "Trained" Grangaard Strategy™ Advisor

If you are looking for a financial professional to help you develop, refine, and implement your plan, you will find resources in the Appendix, along with the address of a website that has a list of advisors in your area who have been trained by my company.

PART ONE

New Realities

1

A New Way to Deal with Changing Realities

This book is about a new way to deal with the changing realities you face in retirement today. You can't do things the way they've always been done because you're living in a different world than your parents and grandparents. You need new strategies that fit new realities and you need to know how to implement those strategies.

Seeing the Big Picture

To understand how to manage money during retirement you have to start by putting retirement into perspective. Many people assume they can think of their life in two phases—the preretirement phase and the retirement phase. Unfortunately, it isn't quite that simple. Both the preretirement phase and the retirement phase have to be broken down into a number of different periods as shown in Illustration 1.

The Accumulation Phase

The preretirement, or Accumulation Phase, is separated into an "Early" Accumulation Period and a "Late" Accumulation Period. The "early" period relates to the majority of your working years when you are focused primarily on accumulating assets for retirement. The "late" period covers the years just prior to retirement when you have to start thinking about repositioning your investments to generate the safe, steady, dependable income you will need for the rest of your life.

The "early" period of the Accumulation Phase starts the day you get your first job and ends about five to seven years before retirement. The "late" period is made up of those last five to seven years. During this time you decide when and how much money to set aside for income purposes and how to invest the rest of your assets to go after the growth you may need to support yourself for the rest of your life. It's a critical time because you really have to decide when to change your overall investment approach from a growth-and-accumulation strategy to a growth-and-income strategy—and this decision has very important consequences.

Illustration 1: The Phases of Retirement

Accumulation		Retirement					
Early	Late	Holding Period 1		Holding Period 2		Holding Period 3	
		1a	1b	2a	2b	3a	3b
Age <58	Age 59 to 65	Age 65 to 75		Age 75 to 85		Age 85 to 95	

The Retirement Phase

The Retirement Phase is separated into three ten-year time frames called holding periods. A holding period is simply the length of time you can stay invested in the stock market to go after the growth you may need while reducing the possibility of realizing investment returns that are less than you are reasonably expecting. Although ultimately you have to determine your own investment horizons, ten-year holding periods often serve as a kind of benchmark for today's retirement investors because they tend to take a lot of the risk out of investing in the stock market.

Each of the three holding periods can be further divided into two five-year periods. Often, you will plan to be able to hold your stock market investments for ten years, but actually sell them sooner than that. In fact, deciding when to sell stocks within your holding periods is one of the most important aspects of retirement investing, and you will seldom hang on to them for a full ten years—even though you can if you want to. You might decide to sell stocks in three years, you might decide to sell them in five years, or you might decide to sell them in eight years—you can never be sure in advance. It all depends upon what's happening in the stock market while you're retired.

Accumulating Assets First

Throughout your working life you accumulate assets for retirement. Then, as you approach age fifty-nine or sixty, you move into the "late" period of the Accumulation Phase in which you ultimately decide when to create your first Income Ladder. You normally have to make this decision sometime within the five to six years before you retire because you need to have your income ready to go as soon as you stop receiving a paycheck. The Income Ladder investments you create are designed to help you do that.

Creating Your First Income Ladder

Income Ladders are the lower-risk, lower-return part of your portfolio that provides the safe, steady, dependable income you need during retirement. They are more of a "process" or "technique" than they are a "thing." They can be constructed in a variety of ways—but they almost always rely on fixed-income investments like bonds, CDs, or immediate annuities to provide the financial resources you need to pay the bills and enjoy yourself after you stop working.

You may wonder why you will probably create your first Income Ladder before you retire. You never know in advance when you will do it, but as you approach retirement you do know that you will have to create an Income Ladder fairly soon. If you are still heavily invested in the stock market, like many people are at that time, this is just another way of saying that you know you are getting close to the point at which you will be forced to sell some stock market investments to get the money you need to create your Income Ladder. Since you never want to be forced to sell stocks when the market is down, and because you have no idea about what will be happening in the market during the rest of the years prior to retirement, you always want to be on the lookout for a good time to sell—just like you will be for the rest of your life.

Making Your First Stock Sales

Ultimately, you have to decide when to create your first Income Ladder and then sell some of your stock market investments. Or, if you have other assets that you want to use first—such as real estate, collectables, or other kinds of investments, you can sell them instead. You use the proceeds from the sale of stocks or other assets to purchase fixed-income securities to build your first Income Ladder. Then, the rest of your assets can stay invested, or be invested, in a diversified portfolio of stock market investments. If you prefer, you can always leave them invested in other assets as well—it's up to you. We focus on stocks because they tend to be more typical of the investments people bring with them into retirement. But everyone's life is different.

Spending Your Income Ladders

As your stock market or other investments are allowed to grow, you spend your Income Ladders to provide the lifestyle you need and want. By about age seventy-five you will probably exhaust the first Income Ladder and need to create a new one to provide the income you need for the next ten years. To do that, you will be able to sell some more of your stock market investments and use the proceeds to purchase new Income Ladder investments. The rest of your assets can then remain invested in the stock market where they are planned to continue growing at the higher rates of return you are reasonably expecting.

You use the same process over and over again to generate both the income and growth you need to maintain your lifestyle throughout retirement. As shown in Illustration 2, you should always have some of your money in Income Ladders for income, and some in the stock market for growth, and hopefully have a reasonable amount left over at the end.

Outdated Ideas About Retirement Financial Management

A number of issues arise because you are likely to end up with a decent amount of money at the end of your life if you manage it this way. You've probably seen the bumper stickers that say something like "Ha, Ha, we're out spending our kid's inheritance!" stuck on the back of camper rigs running up and down the freeways—or heard the old saying that the best retirement plan will have you "spending your last dollar on your last day." These are cute little sayings as long as you keep in mind that they're just for fun—because the reality is much different. This kind of thinking may have worked in the old days when you didn't live very long in retirement, but it's unlikely to work today.

If you do a good job taking care of yourself during retirement there will probably be a fair amount of money left over at the end of your life, and the question is, what do you want to do with it? Do you want to give it to charity? Do you want to give it

Illustration 2: The Grangaard Strategy™ (A Conceptual Overview)

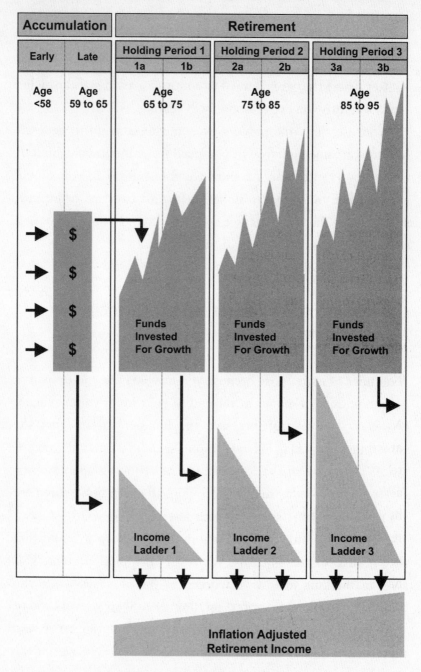

to the church? Do you want to find a way to get as much as possible to your children and grandchildren? These are very important questions that may never even come up if you simply plan to
manage your money the old-fashioned way—because there probably won't be much left to worry about anyway.

But if you manage your money the way I suggest, there may
be quite a bit left over, and you will certainly want to decide
what to do with it. You will find that after getting your retirement house in order, the next step is usually to start working on
your estate plan.

The IRS and the Minimum Required Distribution Rules

Making this whole process a bit more complicated is the fact that
at a certain age the Internal Revenue Service actually forces you
to start taking money out of your retirement plans and IRA
accounts—whether you want to or not. They do this because you
have to pay income taxes when the money comes out. These
required withdrawals are usually referred to as "minimum
required distributions" and they define when and how much you
have to take out of your accounts.

You need to keep these rules in mind when you start thinking
about creating Income Ladders later in life. Sometimes you actually have to plan to take out more money than you need just to
satisfy these regulations. The trouble is, because of the way the
minimum distribution amounts are calculated, it's impossible to

know in advance how much you will have to take out each year—so it's a big part of the overall management process later in retirement. It's also an area where your advisors will play an important role, because calculating these amounts can be a little tricky sometimes—and you don't want to make a mistake.

Tax-Deferred Investing and the "Liquidity Tax"

Another thing to keep in mind is that throughout the book we assume that you don't have to pay income taxes each time you sell stock market investments to create Income Ladders. We assume that you will be able to defer these taxes until you actually take money out of your accounts. This will only be true if you are managing your investments inside of tax-deferred vehicles like retirement plans, IRAs, annuity contracts, and certain kinds of investment trusts.

If you are invested in taxable accounts you will probably have to pay income and/or capital gains taxes every time you sell stock market investments to create Income Ladders. I call this the "liquidity tax" and we will talk a lot more about it. If you are forced to pay this tax over and over throughout a long retirement period you probably won't be able to generate nearly as much income. So whenever possible, you may want to get your retirement assets into tax-deferred accounts so you can take advantage of the potential tax benefits and income-generating opportunities they can provide.

Don't Use Outdated Approaches

You face new realities today as a retiree. The game has changed and you have to change with it. For a lot of reasons we will be talking about, you simply can't plan to "spend your last dollar on your last day"—and as an investor, you also can't afford to allow yourself to get caught up in the "heat of the moment."

Retirement investors often vacillate between the twin perils of investing too conservatively on the one hand and too aggressively on the other. As often as not we lurch back and forth between the extremes based upon what has happened most recently in the stock market. If things have gone well, we're tempted to put too much into the stock market, and if they haven't gone so well our tendency is to become too conservative. The goal is to stop vacillating. You need to make good, long-term, strategic decisions rather than getting whipsawed every time the markets move for or against you.

It's often said that the stock market is driven by "fear" and "greed." You absolutely cannot let these emotions control your investment behavior in retirement. You need to learn how to "thread the financial needle" by having the "right amount" invested in Income Ladders and the "right amount" invested in the stock market—and by managing the balance wisely over time.

Find a Qualified Financial Professional

As you have probably gathered by now, retirement is not a good time for do-it-yourself financial management—although you will obviously play a very crucial role. It's important to find a qualified financial professional to help you pull it all together. What we teach you in this book will help you become a more informed financial consumer, but as much as I would like to think otherwise, the book alone is not enough. The tax complexities alone make it imperative to get some expert assistance. It's just like going to the doctor. You need to know something about what ails you, but at some point you have to put yourself into the hands of a pro. Let's face it—you're not going to do your own surgery.

2

Plan to Live Longer

The whole idea behind the Twelve Principles of Twenty-First-Century Retirement Investing is to help you get the income you need in retirement—and one of the most important things to understand about retirement investing today is that you're probably going to have to maintain that income for longer and longer retirement periods. Increasing life expectancies are one of the main reasons you need new and better ways to manage your money during retirement. Since you are likely to be living longer, you either have to accumulate more money, do a better job managing the money you have, or both.

You also have to understand that you can't plan for average life expectancies. Since you are probably going to be living longer during retirement you have to create financial plans and develop financial strategies that will help you make your money last a lot longer than it used to—and average life expectancies are usually not long enough.

Expect to Outlive the Averages

The average life expectancy today of a sixty-five-year-old is about twenty years. So if you reach age sixty-five you can plan on average to live to about age eighty-five. But remember, this is just an average—and averages can be very misleading. If the average life expectancy is twenty years, approximately half of us won't live that long, while the other half will live even longer.

Averages can give you a good "feel" for the overall probabilities, but you can't actually plan to live that long. When it comes to your own life you have to plan much more realistically for what could actually happen to you. In fact, we all have to plan to live longer than average. I tell people in my retirement planning seminars that a realistic guideline is to plan to live until at least age ninety-five—because many of us will.

It's important to know this because many financial planners and most financial planning software programs use average life expectancies. Many of them expect you to decide "when you want to run out of money." Often, the averages are suggested as a way to help you make this decision. But can you really plan to die on cue? Of course not—and therefore you can't plan to run out of money on cue either. You have no idea how long you will live in retirement and therefore you have to make sure your money never runs out. You have to follow Principle #1: Expect to Outlive the Averages. If you plan for average life expectancies you may be making a real mistake right from the start.

The Older You Get, the Older You Are Likely to Get

One of the most interesting things about life expectancies is that the longer you live the more likely it is that you will live even longer. As strange as it may sound, we are a lot like refrigerators in this regard.

Many years ago my wife and I were buying our first home and my father was lending us the down payment. After doing a walk-through of the house I realized that the refrigerator was very old, so I figured we would need to buy a new one. I called my dad to see if he could sweeten the pot a little bit and he asked me how old the refrigerator was. I told him it looked like it was about twenty years old, although I didn't really know for sure. He responded that if a refrigerator has lasted twenty years it will probably last another twenty. I think he said, "If it's got a good compressor, it's got a good compressor," or something like that. We didn't replace it for five or six years.

Like the old refrigerator, we all have to plan to keep getting older as we get older—and the surprising reality is that you don't lose a year of life expectancy for each year you live. At age 85 your average life expectancy is about seven years. If you live to age 90 your average life expectancy drops to about five years. So as you can see in Illustration 3, you can live an additional five years and yet only give up about two years of life expectancy!

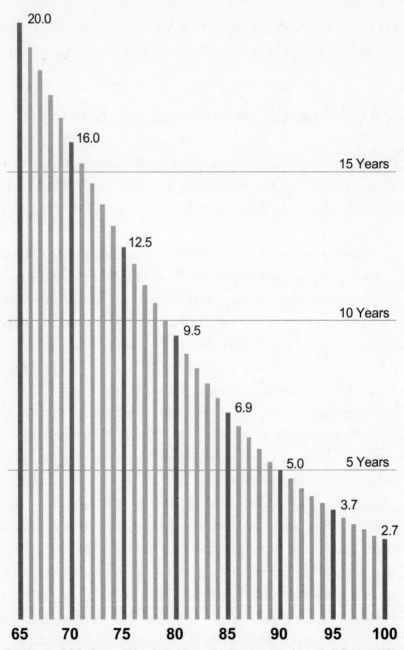

Illustration 3: Average Life Expectancies for People Age 65 and Older

20.0

16.0

15 Years

12.5

10 Years

9.5

6.9

5.0   5 Years

3.7

2.7

65   70   75   80   85   90   95   100

Data Source: IRS Publication 590, Individual Retirement Arrangements, Appendix E, Table 1, 1999

Illustration 4: Percentage of People Still Living at Age 65 and Older

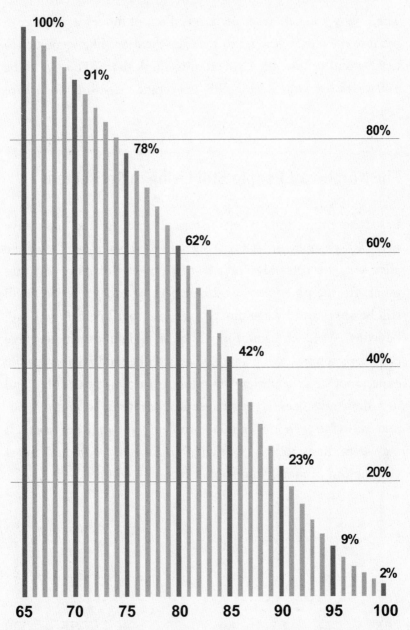

Data Source: US Dept. of Health and Human Services, Nat'l Center for Health Statistics, 1998

That's why you can never plan to run out of money at any age—because the closer you get to that age the more likely you are to live beyond it. It's rather sobering to think that if you live to be 100 years old your average life expectancy is still almost three years.

The Number of People Still Living in Retirement

Based on projections using historical data, at age eighty-five over 40 percent of today's sixty-five-year-olds will still be alive—so you certainly don't want to be out of money at that point. At age ninety almost 25 percent of today's retirees will still be alive, and by age ninety-five close to 10 percent will still be living. As Illustration 4 makes clear, a significant percentage of today's retirees will probably live well beyond an average life expectancy. As healthier lifestyles, better medical care, and incredible advances in pharmaceuticals continue to improve our odds of living even longer, this "problem" will only get worse. It may seem funny to think of living longer as a "problem," but if you run out of money too soon it certainly will be.

3

Plan for the "Right Amount" of Income

Living longer is a good thing, but it can be a real financial challenge for you and your family. Not only will your income needs fluctuate throughout longer retirement periods, but the longer you live, the greater your exposure will be to inflation. So you not only need to make your money last a lot longer, you also have to account for changing income needs and attempt to overcome the drag of inflation.

Adjusting for Inflation

It's important to get a feel for how inflation rates have varied over the years because you will have to decide what rates to use in your own plan—and small changes can have a dramatic impact. Many people tend to stick close to the long-run average of about 3 percent for planning purposes, but you should also have a feel for the consequences of using different rates.

Based upon data constructed by the U.S. Department of Labor, Bureau of Labor Statistics, concerning the Consumer Price Index for All Urban consumers (CPI-U), in the 25 years between 1976 and 2000 inflation averaged 4.7 percent—which is extremely high for such a long period of time. Many of you may remember the oil embargoes, wage and price controls, stagflation, high unemployment, high interest rates and all the other problems that plagued us in the '70s and '80s. All combined, they led to a twenty-five-year average annual rate of inflation that was well above the more normal 3.1 percent long-term rate.

In the ten years between 1991 and 2000 inflation moderated substantially, averaging only 2.7 percent per year, while during the five years between 1996 and 2000 it actually came down as low as 2.5 percent. In fact, in the last few years, we have seen some of the lowest inflation rates we've had in a very long time. Keep in mind—these are historical rates, and as I caution many times throughout the book, past performance is not a guarantee of future results. But the lessons from the past are all we really have to go on—as imperfect a predictor as they may be.

The Importance of Protecting Yourself Against Inflation

At both the ten-year and five-year average annual inflation rates, the cost of a loaf of bread will more than double during a typical

Illustration 5: The Impact of Inflation During Retirement Using
Historical Inflation Rate Assumptions

Cost of a Loaf of Bread

Actual Historical Data			Projections (Loaf of Bread)			
Time Period	# of Years	Ave. %	Cost Today	10 Years	20 Years	30 Years
1926 to 2000	75	3.1%	$2.50	$3.39	$4.60	$6.25
1951 to 2000	50	4.0%	$2.50	$3.70	$5.48	$8.11
1976 to 2000	25	4.7%	$2.50	$3.96	$6.26	$9.92
1991 to 2000	10	2.7%	$2.50	$3.26	$4.26	$5.56
1996 to 2000	5	2.5%	$2.50	$3.20	$4.10	$5.24

Source: Calculated by Paul Grangaard using data presented in *Stocks, Bonds, Bills and Inflation®
2001 Yearbook,* © 2001 Ibbotson Associates, Inc. Based on copyrighted works by Ibbotson and
Sinquefield. All rights reserved. Used with permission.
Based upon U.S. Department of Labor, Bureau of Labor Statistics, Consumer Price Index for All
Urban Consumers (CPI-U). For Illustration purposes only. Past performance is not a guarantee
of future results.

thirty-year retirement period. Illustration 5 shows the projected
cost of a loaf of bread at ten-year intervals using some of the historical inflation rates that we've actually experienced over different portions of the last seventy-five years. As you can see, they
bounced around all over the place depending upon the period
considered.

Spend a few minutes reviewing the historical data and hypothetical projections to get a feel for what has actually happened
in the past and for what could potentially happen again in the
future. Think of everything you buy on a day-to-day basis and

consider how these historical inflation rates would impact their prices during an extended retirement period. You will begin to get a much clearer picture of how important it is to manage your portfolio to protect yourself against these inevitable price increases.

Maintaining an Overall Lifestyle in Retirement

Remember, inflation simply increases the price of everything—it forces you to have more money to purchase the same quantity of goods and services. In other words, to maintain any given lifestyle you need more and more income each year just to stay in the same place.

Using the long-run seventy-five-year average annual inflation rate of 3.1 percent, a $20,000 current lifestyle would require $27,140 in ten years, $36,830 in twenty years, and $49,979 in thirty years—an increase of almost 150 percent. At a 4 percent average annual inflation rate you would need to increase your retirement income by more than 200 percent over a typical thirty-year retirement period, from $20,000 all the way up to $64,868—just to maintain a $20,000 lifestyle. At the twenty-five-year average annual rate of 4.7 percent, your need for income would increase by almost 300 percent, from $20,000 in the first year to $79,329 in the thirtieth year. And of course, as you can see in Illustration 6, you wouldn't need nearly as much income if you assumed the lower average annual rates of inflation from the latest ten-year and five-year periods.

Illustration 6: The Impact of Inflation During Retirement
Using Historical Inflation Rate Assumptions

Maintaining a Lifestyle

Actual Historical Data			Projections ($20,000 Lifestyle)			
Time Period	# of Years	Ave. %	Cost Today	10 Years	20 Years	30 Years
1926 to 2000	75	3.1%	$20,000	$27,140	$36,830	$49,979
1951 to 2000	50	4.0%	$20,000	$29,605	$43,822	$64,868
1976 to 2000	25	4.7%	$20,000	$31,659	$50,115	$79,329
1991 to 2000	10	2.7%	$20,000	$26,106	$34,075	$44,478
1996 to 2000	5	2.5%	$20,000	$25,602	$32,772	$41,951

Source: Calculated by Paul Grangaard using data presented in *Stocks, Bonds, Bills and Inflation®*
2001 Yearbook, © 2001 Ibbotson Associates, Inc. Based on copyrighted works by Ibbotson and
Sinquefield. All rights reserved. Used with permission.
Based upon U.S. Department of Labor, Bureau of Labor Statistics, Consumer Price Index for All
Urban Consumers (CPI-U). For Illustration purposes only. Past performance is not a guarantee
of future results.

You Will Not Be Working Overtime in Retirement

The important thing to realize is that even at the very low historical inflation rate of 2.5 percent over the last five years, you
would still need to double your income over a typical thirty-year
retirement period just to maintain your lifestyle. And think
about this—during retirement you will not be getting cost-of-
living increases or merit raises at work, because you will be
retired. You will not be increasing your billing rate, working
more overtime, taking on additional jobs, or doing any of the

other things you did, or that were done for you, to offset rising prices while you were working. The only way you will be able to protect yourself against the effects of inflation is to manage your money more effectively during retirement.

Fluctuating Retirement Income Needs

Once you understand the potential impact of inflation you can start planning for your retirement income. Many people assume that retirement income planning simply means computing a percentage of their preretirement salary and increasing it each year for inflation. This is the approach used by many of the commercially available financial planning programs and by some financial advisors. It might work for certain people, but the reality is usually much different.

During retirement your income needs can fluctuate substantially from year-to-year, so a straight-line income approach, even if it is adjusted for inflation, is often not the most realistic way to plan. It's the simplest approach for sure, but not necessarily the best.

For example, one of the things that always comes up in discussions about retirement income planning is the idea that you may need less income in later years than you do in earlier years—because as you age, so the theory goes, you tend to spend less. There is some truth in this perspective, but of course it applies differently to everyone. Unfortunately, there aren't any standard "income reduction percentages" that you can apply at various ages to compute your own individual lifestyle needs. There are plenty of old rules of thumb still floating around—but you don't want to rely on them.

And then there is always the opposite issue of whether or not you might actually experience increasing costs during retirement. Think of prescription drugs, health care, medical and long-term care insurance, assisted living, nursing home care, and so on. For every person who thinks their living expenses will go down later in life you can find someone else who will argue persuasively that theirs will actually go up.

Reasons Your Income Needs Can Fluctuate

You need to think about whether you want to buy into this income-reduction theory or not. Accepting a theory in general terms is one thing. Building it into your retirement plan is something else altogether. In general it's probably reasonable to plan for a little less in later years—but how much less is a matter for you to decide for yourself. At any rate, the whole debate points out that the idea of planning to spend the same amount each year, even if it is adjusted for inflation, may be a little too simplistic for many of us.

There are plenty of other reasons your income needs can fluctuate over the years—some that you can plan for and some that you can't. But you should always do your best to proactively account for the things you can anticipate. You obviously can't plan for everything—events happen in your life that cannot be predicted. Changing medical circumstances and living arrangements, changing hobbies and interests, births, deaths, marriages, divorces, changes in the economic circumstances of your children and grandchildren, and so many other uncertainties make it virtually impossible to plan for everything. Over the course of a thirty-year retirement period you are going to run into all sorts of unanticipated situations that require constant adjustment and accommodation. That's just the way life is, and you can't change it with a retirement plan and a little wishful thinking.

Keeping Your Retirement Plans Flexible

But you can keep your retirement plans as flexible as possible. A good plan is not, and never should be, a straitjacket. You shouldn't sacrifice flexibility for structure. You need both. You need to create retirement plans that provide as much structure and flexibility as you can get. They need to let you take into account all of the variables you can predict while also being able to handle the ones you can't. For example, you might decide that you want to plan for decreasing amounts of income during retirement while also deciding to take more expensive vacations in the early years and to help a child or grandchild with college later on. Or, you may want to include additional expenses for home repairs while also accounting for the fact that you will eventually pay off a mortgage. The bottom line is that creating a more accurate and more flexible retirement plan often requires a more detailed budget.

Providing for Fluctuating Income Needs

Think about how you manage your financial affairs before you retire. You earn a certain amount of income that generally goes up with inflation each year. You probably also get merit raises that keep your real income growing over time. For many people this takes place in a fairly predictable, step-by-step fashion. But you probably also encounter circumstances in which you need to spend more or less than you make in any particular year— perhaps for a down payment on a house, or maybe to purchase a car or a cabin. Generally, you have to deal with these fluctuating income needs by saving money in some years, and spending it in other years. Most of us are more than familiar with the process.

You can do the same thing in retirement. You can create a regular stream of income, put some of it away in the years you don't need it all, and use some of it in the years when you need a little extra. However, in retirement you have much more flexibility, because you are able to create and adjust your income streams at many different times and in many different ways—depending on the length of your holding periods and how often you sell stocks. Throughout retirement you have a lot of opportunities to modify your "regular" stream of income, which can give you a great deal of control and flexibility to meet changing circumstances.

A Sample Retirement Budget

When you create a retirement plan you will probably start with your "base income requirements," which in Illustration 7 begin at $50,000 per year and drop to $30,000 over a thirty-year retirement period. This is simply the amount you need to support your overall lifestyle before making adjustments for special items you want to consider separately.

Converting from Purchasing Power to Inflation-Adjusted Income

Your "base income requirements" refer to your core lifestyle expenses—things like mortgages, property taxes, utilities, food, clothing, car payments, gas, entertainment, gifts, and so on—and, along with the special items, are initially stated in terms of current purchasing power.

Once you've identified your "base income" needs and any special adjustments you want to consider, you can determine how much purchasing power you need each year. Most people are surprised to see how much it fluctuates—even with just a few special items. It jumps around a lot from year to year as the "base income" needs change and various adjustments come and go.

Ultimately, however, both the "base income" and the special adjustment amounts have to be converted into future, inflation-adjusted dollars. When you do your planning you usually start by figuring out how much income you need each year in terms of

Illustration 7: Planning for Flexible Retirement Income Needs

Year	Base Income	Extra Travel	College Tuition	Home Repair	Prelim Total	Inflation Adjust	Mortgage Payment	Final Income
1	$50,000	$15,000			$65,000	$0		$65,000
2	$50,000				$50,000	$1,500		$51,500
3	$50,000	$15,000			$65,000	$3,959		$68,959
4	$50,000				$50,000	$4,636		$54,636
5	$50,000	$15,000		$5,000	$70,000	$8,786		$78,786
6	$50,000				$50,000	$7,964		$57,964
7	$50,000	$15,000			$65,000	$12,613		$77,613
8	$50,000				$50,000	$11,494		$61,494
9	$50,000	$15,000			$65,000	$17,340		$82,340
10	$50,000			$5,000	$55,000	$16,763	($12,000)	$59,763
11	$40,000		$10,000		$50,000	$17,196	($12,000)	$55,196
12	$40,000		$10,000		$50,000	$19,212	($12,000)	$57,212
13	$40,000		$10,000		$50,000	$21,288	($12,000)	$59,288
14	$40,000		$10,000		$50,000	$23,427	($12,000)	$61,427
15	$40,000		$10,000	$5,000	$55,000	$28,192	($12,000)	$71,192
16	$40,000				$40,000	$22,319	($12,000)	$50,319
17	$40,000				$40,000	$24,188	($12,000)	$52,188
18	$40,000				$40,000	$26,114	($12,000)	$54,114
19	$40,000				$40,000	$28,097	($12,000)	$56,097
20	$40,000			$5,000	$45,000	$33,908	($12,000)	$66,908
21	$30,000				$30,000	$24,183	($12,000)	$42,183
22	$30,000				$30,000	$25,809	($12,000)	$43,809
23	$30,000				$30,000	$27,483	($12,000)	$45,483
24	$30,000				$30,000	$29,208	($12,000)	$47,208
25	$30,000			$5,000	$35,000	$36,148	($12,000)	$59,148
26	$30,000				$30,000	$32,813	($12,000)	$50,813
27	$30,000				$30,000	$34,698	($12,000)	$52,698
28	$30,000				$30,000	$36,639	($12,000)	$54,639
29	$30,000				$30,000	$38,638	($12,000)	$56,638
30	$30,000			$5,000	$35,000	$47,480	($12,000)	$70,480

what that income will buy today, and then adjust it to reflect future inflationary price increases. In other words, you budget as if you were going to pay for everything today and then calculate the effect of inflation to determine how much more you need to be able to pay for it all in the future.

As you probably expect, the inflation adjustments tend to increase with time. In fact, in later years, the inflation adjustment amounts are often actually greater than the amounts of purchasing power they are intended to protect. Even at the long-run average annual inflation rate of 3 percent—which is a reasonably conservative planning estimate today, you can see that compounded inflation over long retirement periods can have a dramatic effect on your need for income.

Other Possible Adjustments

Another thing to keep in mind is that some of the special items might need to be adjusted with different inflation rates. For example, recent increases in higher education costs have far outpaced the average rate of inflation in the overall economy. If you plan to inflation-protect the amount of income you need for college tuition ten years from now, you might want to increase that particular item at more than the average 3 percent inflation rate used for the rest of your expenses. The same may be true for other special items as well.

Some Special Items That Don't Get Adjusted for Inflation

There is another type of special adjustment you should consider. A good example is your mortgage payment. People often pay off a mortgage during retirement. If you do that, you will probably no longer need the income that was used in previous years to make the payment. As a result, you may be able to reduce your income requirements by that amount each year without causing any change in your overall lifestyle.

However, the mortgage amount should be subtracted from your budget after you make the inflation adjustment each year. The mortgage payment is a fixed monthly amount, so, unlike most other expenses, it doesn't increase with inflation. The payments never change—regardless of the inflation rate. Subtracting the mortgage payments before you make the inflation adjustments would assume that inflation somehow affects your mortgage—which it doesn't. You have to pay close attention to these kinds of distinctions when following Principle #2: Adjust for Changing Income Needs, because they can make a big difference in your overall retirement income planning.

PART TWO

Managing Your Retirement Resources

4

Replace Your Paycheck

One of the first things you need to figure out in retirement is where your income is going to come from. In essence, you need to replace your paycheck. You need to set yourself up with safe, steady, dependable income before you can make any other investment decisions. Income is not a by-product of your retirement investment strategy. Income is the product. It always comes first. Having your income needs taken care of should give you the flexibility, comfort, and control you need to manage the rest of your retirement investments with patience, prudence, and confidence—just like you did before you retired. That's why the third principle of Twenty-First-Century Retirement Investing is Create Dependable Income for the Rest of Your Life. Until you have your income needs taken care of you are not free to compose the rest of your investment plan.

Sources of Income in Retirement

During retirement you will probably be living on investments, along with Social Security, pensions, and any other sources of income you may have. The Grangaard Strategy™ focuses exclusively on *your* retirement investments—like retirement plans at work, IRAs, annuities, and so on. In fact, managing *your* assets during retirement is what this book is all about. The other sources of income, like Social Security and pensions, are certainly important, and in some cases may even be the primary source of retirement income for some people—like my father. You obviously need to take all of them into account in your overall retirement planning. But they are different for everybody, and they are not the focus of this book.

Some people have pensions and some don't. Some have other sources of income—like rental property and other business interests, and some don't. But almost all of us will have retirement investments that we have to manage ourselves—and for many, if not most of us, they will be the biggest source of income we have. That's why I focus exclusively on *your* retirement assets. There are plenty of other books available about pensions, Social Security, and other retirement issues. The bookstore shelves are full of them.

Use Income Ladders to Create Dependable Income for the Rest of Your Life

To provide the safe, steady, dependable income you need during retirement you can use an investment strategy called Income Ladders. Income Ladders are a linchpin of successful retirement finance. Not only can they give you the dependable income you need and want, they can also play a crucial role in helping you manage the rest of your investment portfolio—because they are one of the best ways to provide the time you need to make better stock market selling decisions throughout retirement.

In fact, Income Ladders are the foundation upon which you can build your stock market holding periods—and stock market holding periods are key to reducing some of your investment risks during retirement. Income Ladders play a dual role. They can help you replace your paycheck and they can help you create the holding periods you may need to support less risky and more effective retirement investment strategies.

A Definition of Income Ladders: What Are They?

Income Ladders are investment portfolios designed to take care of your income needs during retirement. They are generally constructed with money you set aside in less risky fixed-income investments like single-premium immediate annuities, which can provide dependable income for specific periods of time. You can also build Income Ladders with other kinds of fixed-income investments like bonds or bank certificates of deposit (CDs), which can be structured to provide income very much like annuities—although with some practical limitations. Keep in mind that CD's are FDIC insured up to $100,000, offer a fixed rate of return, and do not necessarily protect against a rising cost of living. The FDIC insurance on CD's applies in the case of bank insolvency, but does not protect market value. The other investments we discuss are not insured and their principal and yield may also fluctuate with market conditions.

Whether you invest in bonds or CDs or take advantage of easy-to-use products like immediate annuities, it's important to understand how Income Ladders work. I'll use bonds in my example because they provide an easy way to illustrate the concept. If you decide to use bonds in your portfolio you will actually have to build your own Income Ladders—or work with an advisor to help you do it, and there may be significant transaction costs associated with the purchase of bonds. If you use annuities, an insurance company will be able to take care of most of it for you—and in some cases may even be able to provide a little extra income as well.

Fixed-Income Investments: A Quick Primer on Bonds

Since I'm going to use bonds to illustrate Income Ladders we'll start with a brief overview. First, what are bonds? Essentially, buying a bond is like making a loan. You give someone your money and they promise to give it back to you at some specific time in the future. However, with bonds, you are usually lending to the government or a big corporation instead of your friends and family.

When you buy a bond, the money you're lending is called the principal, and the date you're supposed to get it back is called the maturity date. If for some reason you don't get the money back when you're supposed to, the bond is said to be in default. All bonds have some default risk, and there are rating services that assess that risk. Prior to the maturity date, bonds are said to be outstanding, which simply means that they haven't matured yet.

While bonds are outstanding, the issuer, or borrower, pays you a certain amount of interest, just like you pay if you borrow money from a bank. The interest rate you earn is stated as a percentage of the face value of the bonds, which is simply the amount of money you get back when the bonds mature. And that's about it. Bonds are pretty simple. You give someone your money, they pay you interest while they have it, and they promise to give it back to you at a particular time in the future.

Income Ladders: How They Work with Bonds

Our example assumes that you want to set aside ten years' worth of safe, steady, dependable income. You won't always use ten-year Income Ladders, but they're fairly common because they give you plenty of time to ride out the ups and downs in the stock market. It's not a coincidence that we use ten-year Income Ladders and therefore ten-year holding periods in retirement, because ten-year investment horizons can help you reduce many of the risks associated with being a stock market investor.

In the example, our Income Ladder will consist of a portfolio of $225,829 worth of individual bonds with a variety of maturity dates. Some mature in one year, some in two years, some in three years and so on. We purchase the bonds with different maturity dates because we want to be able to spend both interest and principal annually throughout the ten-year period. By combining the value of the bonds maturing at the end of each year with the interest earned on all of the bonds that year we should be able to provide the income we need for the following year.

Increasing Income in Retirement: Compensating for Inflation

It may seem at the bottom of the Income Ladder example in Illustration 8 that we're trying to provide an increasing annual standard of living—but we're not. To maintain the same lifestyle, our income has to go up with inflation, so our Income Ladders are built to produce more and more income each year. If you assume an average annual inflation rate of 3 percent per year, maintaining a $25,000 lifestyle requires almost $33,000 in ten years—an increase of more than 30 percent!

Illustration 8: Income Ladder of Treasury Bonds

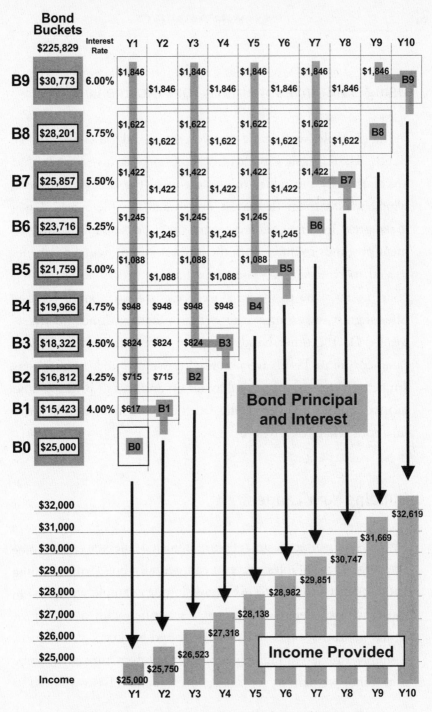

For illustration purposes only. Not representative of an actual investment.

Using Safer Investments in Your Income Ladders

In the example, we assume that you invest only in U.S. Treasury Bonds. U.S. Treasury Bonds are fixed-income investments that are backed by the full faith and credit of the U.S. government, which makes them the safest investments in the world. They make great Income Ladder investments because the U.S. government promises to make both the interest and principal payments if held to maturity—so you never have to worry about getting your money. Due to their reduced risk, treasury bonds tend to offer slightly lower interest rates than other fixed-income investments. On the other hand, investing in higher-yielding, lower-rated corporate bonds (commonly known as "junk bonds") has a much greater risk of price fluctuation and loss of principal and income than U.S. government securities. So you need to be careful about what you invest in.

Building Your Ladder

After establishing your inflation-adjusted income needs and deciding what to invest in, you can actually build your Income Ladder. Since we plan to use bonds in our example we will purchase an assortment of individual securities with a variety of annual maturity dates—I call them "bond buckets." A "bucket" is simply a bunch of individual bonds that all mature at the same time. Since we plan to get income on an annual basis we need to purchase bonds with nine different maturity dates. That way, you can spend some of the principal each year.

The total amount of bonds you put into each bucket depends on interest rates and when you plan to use the principal. At a 6 percent interest rate, the $30,773 worth of bonds in Bucket 9 earn $1,846 of interest for nine years and are then used for income in year ten. At a 4.5 percent rate, the $18,322 worth of bonds in Bucket 3 earn $824 of interest for three years and are then used for income in year four. The total amount of bonds in all the buckets—$225,829, plus all the interest on all the bonds, should take care of your income needs for the entire ten-year period.

The amount of income you need, the inflation rate you use, the interest rates you expect to earn, and the amount of bonds in each bucket are unique in each situation. Often, you have to sell other assets to get the money you need to buy the bonds, or reinvest existing fixed-income investments to get the interest rates and maturity dates you require. But it's extremely important that you do create the Income Ladders—so you have to get the money somewhere. It's one of the only ways you can make sure you will have the income you need when you need it. Most people sell stock market investments to get the money they need to create their Income Ladders—but some people sell other assets as well. However you decide to do it, your advisors can help you sort out the options and analyze your own situation.

Interest Rates

In most cases interest rates are generally higher for longer maturity bonds and lower for shorter maturity bonds. There are many reasons for this—all of which are well beyond the scope of this book. Suffice it to say that on any given day your advisors should be able to help you determine interest rates for bonds of any given maturity—and that normally, the longer-term bonds will have higher interest rates than the shorter-term bonds.

Holding Fixed-Income Investments Until They Mature

An important point that needs to be emphasized is that with Income Ladders we almost always hold our fixed-income investments until they mature. In fact, this is one of the essential features of an Income Ladder—you generally don't sell the investments ahead of schedule. The reason you don't is because your Income Ladders are built to rely on the amount of interest and principal you are expecting to get back each year. The only way you can predict how much you are going to get is to hold your bonds until they mature—because at maturity, you should get back the face value you are expecting—especially if you are investing in U.S. Government Bonds.

What Happens If You Sell Bonds Before They Mature?

What happens if you don't hold your bonds until they mature? When you buy bonds, they come with a promise to pay their face value at maturity. And of course you earn interest on the bonds until that time. What many people don't realize is that because of day-to-day fluctuations in interest rates, the market values of your bonds actually fluctuate like stock market investments. So if you decide to sell a bond before it matures you can never be sure in advance how much you will get for it, because if interest rates go up, the value of the bond goes down.

On the other hand, if interest rates go down, the value of the bond goes up. Although this would seem to be a favorable outcome, you never know for sure if interest rates are going to go up or down after you buy your bonds, and during retirement, you can't afford to take the risk that they will go up.

Investing in Bond Mutual Funds During Retirement

Many people think that bond mutual funds are a good place to invest during retirement. However, they tend not to make good Income Ladder investments—because they never mature. Just like stock market mutual funds, bond funds fluctuate in value on a day-to-day basis. And, unlike the bonds you may have in your own Income Ladders, bond funds as a whole never mature—so you don't have access to the principal of any of the individual bonds in the fund.

If you need some of your principal back each year to provide income during retirement, you will be forced to sell shares of the entire fund at current prices. As a result, you won't be able to predict how much will be available. It will depend on what happens to interest rates while you're retired—which doesn't give you much comfort in the dependability of the income you plan to get out of your portfolio.

You need to keep in mind that all mutual funds, whether stock or bond funds, are investments that fluctuate with market conditions, and involve risk, so that when redeemed, your shares may be worth more or less than original cost. Mutual funds are only available by prospectus, and you should contact your financial advisor or the mutual fund company for a copy of the prospectus for any fund you are interested in. You should always read it carefully before investing or sending money.

How Often Do You Want to Get Your Paycheck During Retirement?

You should also keep in mind that you don't have to get your income at the beginning of each year. In the example, we assumed that you wanted income on an annual basis, but in reality, many people prefer to get their "paychecks" at the beginning of each quarter or even at the beginning of each month.

You can accommodate different income schedules by adding

additional bond buckets to your Income Ladders. For example, if you want to get income on a quarterly basis, you can create thirty-nine quarterly bond buckets instead of nine annual bond buckets. This will provide principal payments at the beginning of each quarter, rather than at the beginning of each year. In this way, you can spend principal and interest on a quarterly basis rather than an annual basis.

Theoretically, you can do the same thing for monthly income too, by adding even more bond buckets. But it starts to get very complicated when you have to build Income Ladders requiring 120 different bond maturities. In fact, it isn't practical at all. Even building quarterly income ladders can get rather complicated. That's why so many people use single-premium immediate annuities for their Income Ladder investments—because they provide income on a monthly basis and get you out from under all the complexity of buying, owning, and managing large portfolios of individual bonds.

Single-Premium Immediate Annuities (SPIAs)

Single-premium immediate annuities, also known as SPIAs, are contracts that you purchase from insurance companies that provide a specific amount of income every month for a specific period of time. The fact that they are "single-premium" annuities simply means that you only pay the insurance company one time, and one amount, for the stream of income they promise to provide. They are "immediate" annuities in the sense that they start paying out monthly income as soon as you buy them.

Obviously, single-premium immediate annuities are a much easier way to get monthly income when compared to going out and buying a hundred or more different bond maturities to create a monthly Income Ladder. Not only that, but many SPIAs today actually offer inflation protection too—so they can provide income each month going up with inflation every year.

With a SPIA, instead of purchasing and managing a portfolio of individual bonds, you simply pay an insurance company a single, lump-sum amount, and they promise to pay you the monthly income you want. Not only do they make things much simpler and easier, they may even provide more income per dollar invested because of the ability of big financial institutions to manage huge fixed-income portfolios much more efficiently and economically than most of us can as individual investors. In essence, when you buy a SPIA, the insurance company is building and managing an Income Ladder for you, and using their financial strength to invest appropriately and back up the payments they promise to make.

SPIAs are not the only kind of annuity that can help you take care of your Income Ladder needs. More and more of the variable annuities offered today provide retirement income options that may also help you replace your paycheck without having to buy and manage complicated portfolios of individual bonds.

Variable Annuities

Variable annuities can be valuable during retirement despite the fact that they generally have additional fees such as mortality and expense risk charges and administrative fees, which are not typically found with other types of investments. Not only do they provide a way for you to protect your investment growth from current taxation, but many of them actually have built-in features that work very much like Income Ladders.

Variable annuities are contracts sold by insurance companies that allow you to invest your money without having to pay income taxes on your investment gains until you take them out during retirement. Your ability to delay paying taxes on your investment earnings can help you accumulate more money. The great thing about variable annuities is that they allow you to invest in a variety of accounts that are invested in the stock market and are often managed by a number of different investment managers—so you can go after higher rates of return in the stock market without being subjected to ongoing taxes.

An important aspect of variable annuities is that through the use of what's called a 1035 exchange, you can move your money from a variable annuity into a SPIA without having to pay income taxes, so you can go after the growth you may need in the stock market and then be able to move the money into an Income Ladder without paying taxes at the time of the conversion. This can help you generate more income during retirement. Please keep in mind that while no taxes or IRS penalties will be incurred, there may be surrender penalties for early withdrawal charged by the issuing insurance company. So you need to do your homework.

Some of the newer variable annuities even have features that make it possible to create your Income Ladders right inside the contract itself. For example, they allow you to take some of your money out of the stock market accounts and turn it into a stream of income for a fixed period of time—just like a SPIA, except that you do it all inside the same contract. This is called "partial term-certain annuitization," and not all contracts allow it—so you have to shop around. Some variable annuities even have guarantees that protect you from fluctuating stock markets by providing minimum rates of return—even on the money you put into stocks. Some of them actually allow you to lock in and protect prior year stock market gains. The combination of these features and a variety of others can make variable annuities an important part of many retirement plans.

Of course, tax-qualified contracts such as an IRA, 401(k), etc., are tax-deferred regardless of whether or not they are funded with an annuity. However, annuities do provide many of these other features and benefits including, but not limited to, guaranteed death benefits and income options, for which mortality and expense risk fees are charged.

There are a few additional things you should always keep in mind when considering annuities. An investment in a variable annuity, like most other investments, involves investment risk, including possible loss of principal. Annuities are designed for long-term retirement investing, and withdrawals of taxable amounts are subject to income tax and, if taken prior to age fifty-nine-and-a-half, a 10 percent federal tax penalty may also apply. Early withdrawals may be subject to withdrawal charges, and annuity contracts, when redeemed, may be worth more or less than the total amount invested. The purchase of a variable annuity can not be required for, and can not be a term of, the provision of any banking service or activity, and an investment in the securities underlying a variable annuity is not guaranteed or endorsed by any bank, is not a deposit or obligation of any bank, and is not federally insured by the FDIC, the Federal Reserve Board or any other federal government agency. Any guarantees offered in an annuity contract are backed by the claims-paying ability of the issuer, so you should always evaluate the financial strength of the issuing company carefully. Obviously, you should always discuss the appropriateness of annuities with a financial professional.

5

Keep Your Kettle Full

During retirement you can replace your paycheck with Income Ladders—but you will probably continue to get your growth from the stock market. Compounding is the engine that drives that growth—both before and during retirement. It also helps your investments have a chance to grow fast enough to keep your Income Ladders replenished throughout longer and longer retirement periods.

Compounding is the process through which you earn investment returns each year on the investment returns from prior years, as well as on the principal amounts you invest. Compounding could be considered as the financial equivalent of a snowball rolling downhill. You start with a small amount of snow that fits into the palm of your hand—which is like your original principal. As that little ball starts rolling down the hill it slowly begins to accumulate more snow—which is like the returns you earn on your principal in the early years of the investment. Then, as it picks up speed and momentum, the original little snowball starts to grow bigger and bigger at a faster and faster rate, accumulating more and more snow on top of the snow it has already accumulated—which is like the investment returns you earn on all the investment returns you earned in prior years. Because of the power of compounding the principal amount you save is usually small compared to your final account balance. It's like the little snowball you held in the palm of your hand compared to the boulder at the bottom of the hill.

Compounding Before Retirement

To understand how important compounding is during retirement consider how important it is before retirement. Assume that you invest $100 per month into a 401(k) plan for forty years. If you earn an 11 percent rate of return each year on the investment—a historical average annual rate of return in the stock market over the last seventy-five years (based upon the total return of the S&P Composite index, which includes five hundred of the largest stocks in the United States from 1957 to the present and ninety of the largest stocks prior to 1957), at the end of forty years the total value of the account will be about $739,129, with your contributions making up only $48,000. As you can see in Illustration 9, the other $691,129, or 93.5 percent of the total accumulated amount, is the compounded growth on the money you invested each month. In other words, if you invest wisely, and get

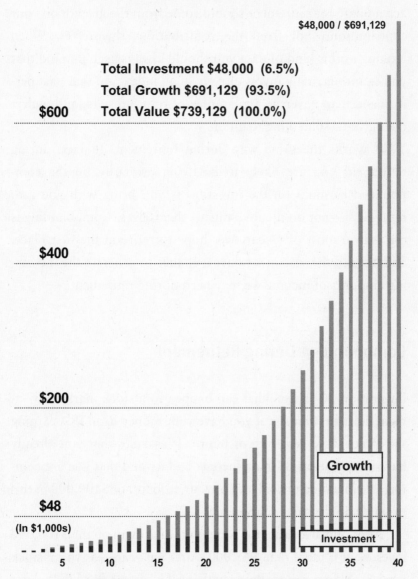

Illustration 9: The Power of Compounding
Growth of $100 per Month for 40 Years at 11% Average Annual Return
(Contributions versus Growth)

$48,000 / $691,129

Total Investment $48,000 (6.5%)
Total Growth $691,129 (93.5%)
$600   Total Value $739,129 (100.0%)

$400

$200

Growth

$48

(In $1,000s)

Investment

5   10   15   20   25   30   35   40

For illustration purposes only. Not representative of an actual investment.
Past performance is not a guarantee of future results.

a reasonable historical rate of return, most of the money you accumulate for retirement should come from the growth on your contributions, not from the contributions themselves. When looking at this kind of data you should always keep in mind that you cannot actually invest directly in an index and that past performance can never be a guarantee of future results, although it does give us something to go on.

It works the same way during retirement. In fact, during retirement you are likely to be living primarily on the compounded earnings on the investments you bring with you into retirement—not on the investments themselves. Compounding is the reason most of us can ever hope to retire in the first place, and it's also the reason we have a chance to generate the increasing amounts of income we may need during retirement.

Compounding During Retirement

Illustration 10 shows what can happen to a stock market investment during retirement if you have your money in an IRA earning the same 11 percent rate of return. It assumes that you already have money set aside in an Income Ladder and that you are comfortable investing the balance of your account, or $100,000 in this example, in the stock market.

After only five years the compounded growth on the $100,000 investment is more than $68,000. After ten years—a typical stock market holding period, the growth itself is almost $184,000. After twenty years, your initial investment will grow to more than

Illustration 10: The Power of Compounding
Comparison of Capital and Growth on
$100,000 at 11% Average Annual Return
for Various Length Investment Periods (During Retirement)

5 Years
Total $168,506

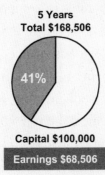

Capital $100,000

Earnings $68,506

10 Years
Total $283,942

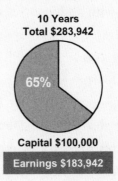

Capital $100,000

Earnings $183,942

15 Years
Total $478,459

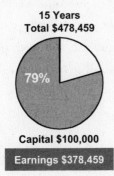

Capital $100,000

Earnings $378,459

20 Years
Total $806,231

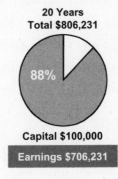

Capital $100,000

Earnings $706,231

25 Years
Total $1,358,546

Capital $100,000

Earnings $1,258,546

30 Years
Total $2,289,230

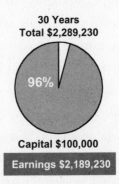

Capital $100,000

Earnings $2,189,230

For illustration purposes only. Not representative of an actual investment.
Past performance is not a guarantee of future results.

$800,000 and after thirty years it will grow to almost $2.3 million—with all but the first $100,000 attributable to compounded earnings.

Of course you will periodically have to use some of the growth from your stock market investments to maintain your income—so you won't be able to leave it all invested for the whole thirty years. During a long retirement period you will probably sell stocks many times to create Income Ladders—sometimes after five years, sometimes after ten years, sometimes after fifteen years, and so on for the rest of your life. However, no matter when you decide to sell, the power of compounding will always be working to your advantage, because as the example makes clear, the balance in your account at the end of any reasonable-length holding period will usually consist largely of compounded growth.

Living on Compounded Returns During Retirement

The important thing to understand is that no matter how long you hold on to your stocks, the earnings on your investments will be growing at a compounded rate. And guess what? That's where your retirement lifestyle is most likely going to come from! After all, how else do you expect to come up with all the money you need to support yourself for thirty-year retirement periods? Many people think that during retirement they are going to live on the money they accumulated for retirement—but the pie charts tell a different story. They make it pretty clear that during retirement you are probably going to be living primarily on the earnings on the money you accumulated prior to retirement, not on the money itself.

Five to 10 Percent of Your Salary Should Cover Your Entire Retirement Lifestyle

The amazing thing about compounding is that by investing as little as 5 to 10 percent of your income while you're working, and earning historical return levels, you should be able to earn, through compounded growth, the other 90 to 95 percent of the money you need to retire. Then, the earnings on that money during retirement should be able to take care of most, if not all of the income you need for the rest of your life. In other words, the growth on your assets before retirement should provide the assets you need to retire in the first place, and the growth on those assets during retirement should be able to provide the income you need for the rest of your life. Essentially, 5 to 10 percent of your earnings, set aside while you are working, managed and invested wisely both before and during retirement, should pretty much take care of the whole retirement problem. So don't make the mistake of thinking that compounding is only important before retirement—because it's clearly important during retirement too. You have to follow Principle #4: Count on Compounding During Retirement to provide the kind of lifestyle you will most likely be looking for.

Compounding Higher Rates of Return

In the examples shown we were able to achieve large increases in our account values because we invested in assets like stock market investments that can reasonably be expected to earn average annual rates of return in the range of 11 percent per year. If we get lower rates of return we won't be able to accumulate as much. Of course that means that we will have less money coming into retirement and less compounded growth during retirement. This will obviously have a negative effect on our overall retirement lifestyle.

Putting Your Money into More Conservative Investments

If you decide to invest more conservatively during retirement, and put the entire $100,000 from the previous example into a vehicle like intermediate-term government bonds, and realize a historical 5.3 percent long-run average annual rate of return (based upon data from *The Wall Street Journal* and the CRSP Government Bond File), you will accumulate far less compounded growth over every five-year period compared with stock market investments. For example, using historical returns, after five years you will have 30 percent more in stocks than in bonds. After ten years you will have 69 percent more in stocks. After twenty years you will have almost 200 percent more in stocks and after thirty years almost 400 percent more.

If you plan to live on growth, like many of us will have to, Illustration 11 shows that it may be difficult to make it work using fixed-income rates of return. Fixed-income investments are a fundamental part of our strategy for building Income Ladders, but they are generally not the way to go for the growth part of our portfolio.

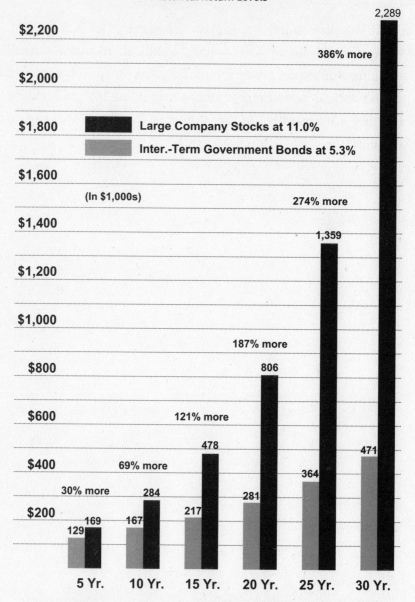

Illustration 11: The Power of Compounding
Accumulated Investment Values
Stocks versus Bonds (Various Investment Periods)
Historical Return Levels

- $2,289
- 386% more
- **Large Company Stocks at 11.0%**
- **Inter.-Term Government Bonds at 5.3%**
- (In $1,000s)
- 274% more
- 1,359
- 187% more
- 806
- 121% more
- 478
- 69% more
- 284
- 30% more
- 364
- 281
- 217
- 471
- 129 169
- 167

5 Yr. 10 Yr. 15 Yr. 20 Yr. 25 Yr. 30 Yr.

Source: Calculated by Paul Grangaard using data presented in *Stocks, Bonds, Bills and Inflation*® *2001 Yearbook*, © 2001 Ibbotson Associates, Inc. Based on copyrighted works by Ibbotson and Sinquefield. All rights reserved. Used with permission.
Large Company Stocks are based on the S&P Composite Index which includes 500 of the largest stocks in the United States from 1957 to the present and 90 of the largest stocks prior to 1957. Intermediate-Term Government Bonds are based primarily on data from *The Wall Street Journal* and the CRSP Government Bond File. For illustration purposes only. Not representative of an actual investment. Past performance is not a guarantee of future results. An investment cannot be made directly in an index. Prices of large company stocks will fluctuate and government bonds are guaranteed by the U.S. government and, if held to maturity, offer a fixed rate of return and fixed principal value.

6

Using History As
Your Guide

One of the most important ideas you need to understand to manage your money properly during retirement is the concept of average annual returns. People in the financial community often refer to them as "geometric returns" and/or "compound average annual returns." However, to keep it simple, I just refer to them as "average annual returns."

Average Annual Returns Defined

An average annual return is simply the rate of return, applied on a consistent, year-to-year basis, which is required to grow an investment from a given starting value to a given ending value over a stated period of time. For example, if you invest $1,000 at the beginning of a ten-year period and at the end of that period have $2,595, you can easily determine the average annual rate of return for the investment. It's simply the one single rate of return, applied consistently, year after year, that would grow the $1,000 investment to $2,595 in ten years. In this example, that one single rate of return is exactly 10 percent per year.

The Importance of Average Annual Returns

The reason average annual returns are so important in retirement planning is that you can use them to compare and evaluate the historical performance of similar investments over different periods of time. You can also use them to compare the performance of different investments over the same period of time. Your ability to compare historical investment results is very important, because having a sense of what has happened in the past will help give you the perspective you need to develop expectations about what might happen in the future. In this book we use historical annual stock and bond market returns as reported in Stocks, Bonds, Bills, and Inflation® 2001 Yearbook by Ibbotson Associates. It is one of the most widely used reference sources for information about historical investment performance.

You Will Never Have a Crystal Ball

You have to keep in mind that the past can never infallibly predict the future. There are always risks involved when you use history as a guide in predicting future investment performance. But it can certainly be helpful to reflect on experience when making these kinds of decisions.

When it comes to retirement planning you have little choice but to develop personal expectations about future investment results—and the challenge is to reduce the possibility that your expectations will be different from what actually happens. The idea of average annual returns will play an important role in that process. In fact, your ability to anticipate investment results with any degree of accuracy is based significantly on the concept of average annual returns.

An Example of Average Annual Returns

Using actual historical performance data for large company stocks, I've set out an actual ten-year investment period from the beginning of 1959 to the end of 1968 in Illustration 12. Large company stocks consist of the 500 largest companies in the United States and are based upon the Standard and Poor's Composite Stock Index—often referred to as the S&P 500® Index.

As the example shows, large company stock returns and investment values fluctuated rather dramatically during this period of time. The best year returned 26.9 percent in 1961 while the worst year lost 10.1 percent in 1966. Over the entire period, however, an initial investment of $1,000 would have grown to an ending balance of $2,595. Although the value of the account went up and down as the annual returns fluctuated from year to year, all in all it was a pretty good ten-year period, with the initial investment more than doubling in value.

Average Annual Returns: The Order Within the Chaos

Despite the fluctuations, there is a fair amount of order underlying the chaos in the stock market. Remember, if you know the beginning value, the ending value, and the number of years in between, you can calculate the average annual rate of return for the whole period—which will give you a pretty good sense of that order.

In fact, $1,000 growing to $2,595 in ten years between 1959 and 1968 is the same as earning 10 percent per year over the same period. The random pattern of ups and downs and the calculated average annual rate of return of 10 percent per year are mathematically the same. As different as they may seem, they get you to exactly the same place. So from an overall investment perspective, these two patterns of returns are essentially interchangeable.

A good way to visualize average annual returns is to look at a graph of actual annual values compared to average annual values. Illustration 13 shows the actual account balances compared to the average account balances for the same ten-year period. The actual value of the investment jumped around all over the place from year to year, and ultimately arrived at an ending balance of $2,595.

Illustration 12: Actual Annual Returns versus Average Annual Returns
10-Year Investment Period from 1959 to 1968
(Large Company Stocks)

Year	Actual Return %	Actual Balance	Average Return %	Average Balance
Balance		$1,000		$1,000
1959	12.0%	$1,120	10.0%	$1,100
1960	0.5%	$1,125	10.0%	$1,210
1961	26.9%	$1,427	10.0%	$1,331
1962	(8.7%)	$1,303	10.0%	$1,464
1963	22.8%	$1,600	10.0%	$1,611
1964	16.5%	$1,863	10.0%	$1,772
1965	12.5%	$2,095	10.0%	$1,949
1966	(10.1%)	$1,885	10.0%	$2,144
1967	24.0%	$2,336	10.0%	$2,358
1968	11.1%	$2,595	10.0%	$2,595

Source: Calculated by Paul Grangaard using data presented in *Stocks, Bonds, Bills and Inflation® 2001 Yearbook*, ©2001 Ibbotson Associates, Inc. Based on copyrighted works by Ibbotson and Sinquefield. All rights reserved. Used with permission.
Large Company Stocks are based on the S&P Composite Index which includes 500 of the largest stocks in the United States. For illustration purposes only. Not representative of an actual investment. Past performance is not a guarantee of future results. An investment cannot be made directly in an index.

But again, underlying the chaos is a smooth 10 percent average annual return line sloping upward and to the right. It illustrates how the average annual rate of return ultimately gets you to the same place, but without all the ups and downs. As you know, it doesn't actually happen this way—but from a mathematical perspective it all amounts to about the same thing. The important point is that behind the random fluctuations there is generally a more predictable pattern of returns. In fact, over longer investment periods, like the ten-year period in the example, there has been a great deal more predictability in the stock market than many people think.

Making Comparisons with Average Annual Returns

You can use average annual returns to compare investment results during this ten-year period with investment results during any other ten-year period. You can also use them to compare this kind of investment—large company stocks in this case, with other kinds of investments over the same period. The actual pattern of ups and downs is less important than the equivalent average annual rate of return for comparison purposes—at least in terms of your ability to use the historical data in your own financial planning.

For example, while the average annual rate of return for large company stocks between 1959 and 1968 was 10 percent, the average annual rate of return for the same stocks between 1988 and 1997 was 18 percent. Obviously, the period from 1988

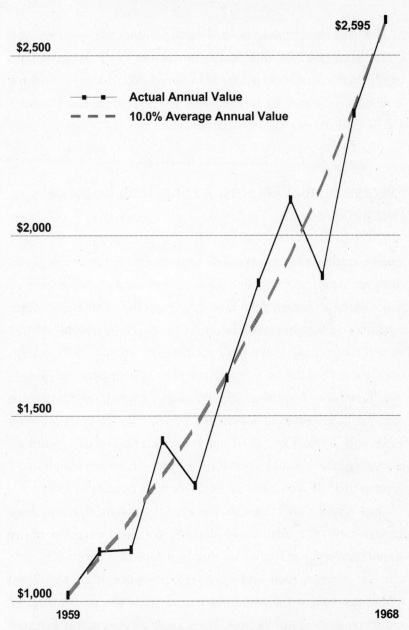

Illustration 13: Actual Annual Returns versus Average Annual Returns
10-Year Investment Period from 1959 to 1968
(Graph of Large Company Stocks)

- ■—■ **Actual Annual Value**
- — — **10.0% Average Annual Value**

$2,595

$2,500

$2,000

$1,500

$1,000

1959   1968

to 1997 was much more rewarding for an investor—but we also know from research that it was much less likely to occur. You would never have wanted to plan for it. You have to plan for "reasonable" rates of return, and 18 percent is not "reasonable"—at least not in historical terms.

Average Annual Returns: A Long-Term Historical Perspective

Understanding average annual returns and how they're calculated can give you a much better appreciation for the importance of maintaining a long-term investment perspective. This is important because you will normally be using long-term historical average annual return data as the basis for making "reasonable" assumptions about the rates of return to use in your own financial plan.

Illustration 14 shows the actual and average annual return data for large company stocks for all seventy-five years between 1926 and 2000. The actual annual returns bounced around all over the place, just like you would expect—between a high of 54 percent in 1933 and a low of negative 43.3 percent in 1931.

But notice that large company stocks produced an average annual rate of return of 11 percent per year over the entire seventy-five-year period. This simply means that earning 11 percent per year in each and every year between 1926 and 2000 would get you to the same place as earning the actual rates of return over the same period. For example, if you had invested

Illustration 14: Actual Annual Returns versus Average Annual Returns
Large Company Stocks
$10 Earning Actual Returns Would Have Grown to $25,865
$10 Earning Average Returns Would Have Grown to $25,865

Year	Actual Return	Average Return	Year	Actual Return	Average Return	Year	Actual Return	Average Return
1926	11.7%	11.0%	1951	24.0%	11.0%	1976	23.8%	11.0%
1927	37.5%	11.0%	1952	18.4%	11.0%	1977	-7.2%	11.0%
1928	43.6%	11.0%	1953	-1.0%	11.0%	1978	6.6%	11.0%
1929	-8.4%	11.0%	1954	52.6%	11.0%	1979	18.4%	11.0%
1930	24.9%	11.0%	1955	31.6%	11.0%	1980	32.4%	11.0%
1931	-43.3%	11.0%	1956	6.6%	11.0%	1981	-4.9%	11.0%
1932	-8.2%	11.0%	1957	-10.8%	11.0%	1982	21.4%	11.0%
1933	54.0%	11.0%	1958	43.4%	11.0%	1983	22.5%	11.0%
1934	-1.4%	11.0%	1959	12.0%	11.0%	1984	6.3%	11.0%
1935	47.7%	11.0%	1960	0.5%	11.0%	1985	32.2%	11.0%
1936	33.9%	11.0%	1961	26.9%	11.0%	1986	18.5%	11.0%
1937	35.0%	11.0%	1962	-8.7%	11.0%	1987	5.2%	11.0%
1938	31.1%	11.0%	1963	22.8%	11.0%	1988	16.8%	11.0%
1939	-0.4%	11.0%	1964	16.5%	11.0%	1989	31.5%	11.0%
1940	-9.8%	11.0%	1965	12.5%	11.0%	1990	-3.2%	11.0%
1941	11.6%	11.0%	1966	-10.1%	11.0%	1991	30.6%	11.0%
1942	20.3%	11.0%	1967	24.0%	11.0%	1992	7.7%	11.0%
1943	25.9%	11.0%	1968	11.1%	11.0%	1993	10.0%	11.0%
1944	19.8%	11.0%	1969	-8.5%	11.0%	1994	1.3%	11.0%
1945	36.4%	11.0%	1970	4.0%	11.0%	1995	37.4%	11.0%
1946	-8.1%	11.0%	1971	14.3%	11.0%	1996	23.1%	11.0%
1947	5.7%	11.0%	1972	19.0%	11.0%	1997	33.4%	11.0%
1948	5.5%	11.0%	1973	-14.7%	11.0%	1998	28.6%	11.0%
1949	18.8%	11.0%	1974	-26.5%	11.0%	1999	21.0%	11.0%
1950	31.7%	11.0%	1975	37.2%	11.0%	2000	-9.1%	11.0%

Source: Calculated by Paul Grangaard using data presented in *Stocks, Bonds, Bills and Inflation® 2001 Yearbook,* © 2001 Ibbotson Associates, Inc. Based on copyrighted works by Ibbotson and Sinquefield. All rights reserved. Used with permission.
Large Company Stocks are based on the S&P Composite Index which includes 500 of the largest stocks in the United States from 1957 to the present and 90 of the largest stocks prior to 1957. For illustration purposes only. Not representative of an actual investment. Past performance is not a guarantee of future results. An investment cannot be made directly in an index.

$10 at the beginning of 1926, you would have accumulated $25,865 by the end of 2000 if you had earned the actual rates of return each year. If you had invested the same $10 at the beginning of 1926 and earned the average annual rate of 11 percent per year, you would have accumulated the same $25,865 by the end of 2000. In other words, the two patterns of returns are essentially the same. They get you to the same place.

Take a few minutes to review the actual annual return data. It will give you a feel for the randomness and unpredictability of large company stock returns and the degree of variability you would have experienced over the last seventy-five years. But also keep in mind that the highly variable seventy-five-year pattern of actual returns would have taken you to the same place as a steady 11 percent average annual rate.

Illustration 15 shows what the long-term historical pattern of annual returns actually looks like, with the steady 11 percent average annual values underlying the significantly fluctuating actual amounts. Of course they both get you to the same $25,865. So while it may have been a roller-coaster ride of ups and downs, it had a strong and easily discernable bias toward positive long-run growth—11 percent per year to be exact.

A History of Small Company Stocks

So far I've focused primarily on large company stocks—but they're not the only game in town. The same average annual return calculations can be made for other segments of the stock

Illustration 15: Cumulative Large Company Stock Values
Actual versus Average Returns (1926 Through 2000)

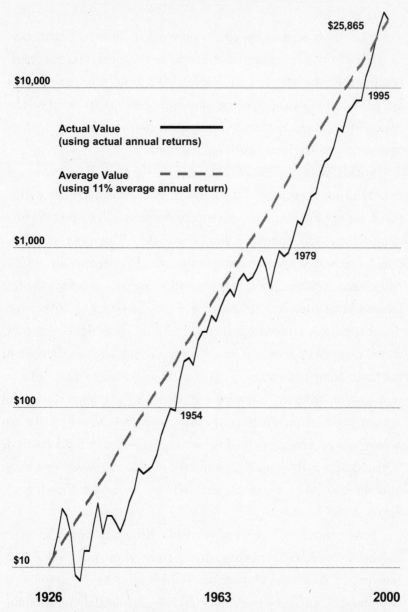

Source: Calculated by Paul Grangaard using data presented in *Stocks, Bonds, Bills and Inflation® 2001 Yearbook,* ©2001 Ibbotson Associates, Inc. Based on copyrighted works by Ibbotson and Sinquefield. All rights reserved. Used with permission.
Large Company Stocks are based on the S&P Composite Index which includes 500 of the largest stocks in the United States from 1957 to the present and 90 of the largest stocks prior to 1957. For illustration purposes only. Not representative of an actual investment. Past performance is not a guarantee of future results. An investment cannot be made directly in an index.

market too, as well as for the bond market. In fact, Illustration 16 provides the actual and average annual return data for small company stocks between 1926 and 2000. Small company stocks are represented by the smallest one-fifth of all stocks listed on the New York Stock Exchange, and they characterize the performance of smaller, faster growing companies.

Notice that small company stocks generated an average annual rate of return of 12.4 percent, but with much more dramatic swings in annual investment performance. The best performance for small company stocks was 142.9 percent in 1933, while the worst year was a negative 58 percent in 1937. Although over the long haul small company stocks outperformed large company stocks by 1.4 percent, it came at the cost of substantially larger fluctuations in value. The highs and lows were far more extreme for small company stocks than they were for large company stocks. This is a clear example of one of the best known rules in investing—in order to get higher average annual rates of return over the long run, you usually have to accept more uncertainty and be willing to invest in markets that fluctuate more dramatically in the short run. However, you may also increase your earnings potential by accepting that higher degree of uncertainty.

Although the 1.4 percent per year difference between large company and small company stocks may seem small, your $10 invested in small stocks back in 1926 would have grown to a whopping $64,022 by the end of 2000—substantially more than the $25,865 you would have earned in large company stocks. That's the difference a small change in your average annual rate

Illustration 16: Actual Annual Returns versus Average Annual Returns
Small Company Stocks
$10 Earning Actual Returns Would Have Grown to $64,022
$10 Earning Average Returns Would Have Grown to $64,022

Year	Actual Return	Average Return	Year	Actual Return	Average Return	Year	Actual Return	Average Return
1926	0.3%	12.4%	1951	7.8%	12.4%	1976	57.4%	12.4%
1927	22.1%	12.4%	1952	3.0%	12.4%	1977	25.4%	12.4%
1928	39.7%	12.4%	1953	-6.5%	12.4%	1978	23.5%	12.4%
1929	-51.4%	12.4%	1954	60.6%	12.4%	1979	43.5%	12.4%
1930	-38.2%	12.4%	1955	20.4%	12.4%	1980	39.9%	12.4%
1931	-49.8%	12.4%	1956	4.3%	12.4%	1981	13.9%	12.4%
1932	-5.4%	12.4%	1957	-14.6%	12.4%	1982	28.0%	12.4%
1933	142.9%	12.4%	1958	64.9%	12.4%	1983	39.7%	12.4%
1934	24.2%	12.4%	1959	16.4%	12.4%	1984	-6.7%	12.4%
1935	40.2%	12.4%	1960	-3.3%	12.4%	1985	24.7%	12.4%
1936	64.8%	12.4%	1961	32.1%	12.4%	1986	6.9%	12.4%
1937	-58.0%	12.4%	1962	-11.9%	12.4%	1987	-9.3%	12.4%
1938	32.8%	12.4%	1963	23.6%	12.4%	1988	22.9%	12.4%
1939	0.4%	12.4%	1964	23.5%	12.4%	1989	10.2%	12.4%
1940	-5.2%	12.4%	1965	41.8%	12.4%	1990	-21.6%	12.4%
1941	-9.0%	12.4%	1966	-7.0%	12.4%	1991	44.6%	12.4%
1942	44.5%	12.4%	1967	83.6%	12.4%	1992	23.4%	12.4%
1943	88.4%	12.4%	1968	36.0%	12.4%	1993	21.0%	12.4%
1944	54.7%	12.4%	1969	-25.1%	12.4%	1994	3.1%	12.4%
1945	73.6%	12.4%	1970	-17.4%	12.4%	1995	34.5%	12.4%
1946	-11.6%	12.4%	1971	16.5%	12.4%	1996	17.6%	12.4%
1947	0.9%	12.4%	1972	4.4%	12.4%	1997	22.8%	12.4%
1948	-2.1%	12.4%	1973	-30.9%	12.4%	1998	-7.3%	12.4%
1949	19.8%	12.4%	1974	-20.0%	12.4%	1999	29.8%	12.4%
1950	38.8%	12.4%	1975	52.8%	12.4%	2000	-3.6%	12.4%

Source: Calculated by Paul Grangaard using data presented in *Stocks, Bonds, Bills and Inflation® 2001 Yearbook*, © 2001 Ibbotson Associates, Inc. Based on copyrighted works by Ibbotson and Sinquefield. All rights reserved. Used with permission.
Small Company Stocks are based on the historical series developed by Professor Rolf W. Banz for 1926 through 1981, and on the Dimensional Fund Advisors (DFA) Small Company 9/10 Fund from 1982 to the present. For illustration purposes only. Not representative of an actual investment. Past performance is not a guarantee of future results. An investment cannot be made directly in an index.

of return can make—and that's why it's so important to follow Principle #5: Invest in the Right Stuff.

Investing for Higher Rates of Return: Creating Larger Accumulations

In fact, to highlight this point, Illustration 17 shows a hypothetical investment of $10,000 growing for thirty years at various average annual rates of return—from 2 percent per year to 12 percent per year. Notice the dramatic differences in accumulated values as we increase the return percentages. For example, if you increase the average annual rate of return from 6 percent to 12 percent you increase the accumulated value of the investment by well over 400 percent, from $57,435 to $299,599, even though you only doubled the rate of return. That's the power of compounding higher average annual rates of return over longer investment periods.

Average Annual Returns for Bonds

Finally, it's worth looking at the actual annual returns and the average annual returns for intermediate-term government bonds. As noted earlier, U.S. government securities, such as U.S. Treasury bonds and bills, are guaranteed by the government for repayment of principal and interest if held to maturity. Illustration 18 shows that intermediate-term government bonds don't

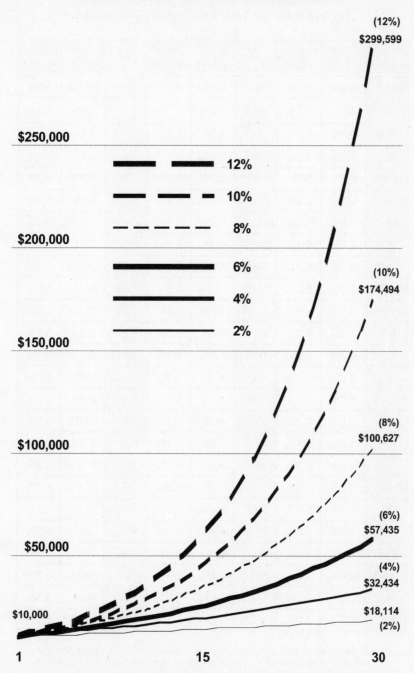

Illustration 17: Average Annual Rate of Return Examples
$10,000 Growing at Rates from 2% to 12%

12%
10%
8%
6%
4%
2%

$250,000
$200,000
$150,000
$100,000
$50,000
$10,000

(12%)
$299,599

(10%)
$174,494

(8%)
$100,627

(6%)
$57,435

(4%)
$32,434

$18,114
(2%)

1   15   30

Returns shown are hypothetical in nature and are for illustration purposes only.
Not representative of an actual investment.

Illustration 18: Actual Annual Returns versus Average Annual Returns
Intermediate-Term Government Bonds

$10 Earning Actual Returns Would Have Grown to $486
$10 Earning Average Returns Would Have Grown to $486

Year	Actual Return	Average Return	Year	Actual Return	Average Return	Year	Actual Return	Average Return
1926	5.4%	5.3%	1951	0.4%	5.3%	1976	12.9%	5.3%
1927	4.5%	5.3%	1952	1.6%	5.3%	1977	1.4%	5.3%
1928	0.9%	5.3%	1953	3.2%	5.3%	1978	3.5%	5.3%
1929	6.0%	5.3%	1954	2.7%	5.3%	1979	4.1%	5.3%
1930	6.7%	5.3%	1955	-0.7%	5.3%	1980	3.9%	5.3%
1931	-2.3%	5.3%	1956	-0.4%	5.3%	1981	9.5%	5.3%
1932	8.8%	5.3%	1957	7.8%	5.3%	1982	29.1%	5.3%
1933	1.8%	5.3%	1958	-1.3%	5.3%	1983	7.4%	5.3%
1934	9.0%	5.3%	1959	-0.4%	5.3%	1984	14.0%	5.3%
1935	7.0%	5.3%	1960	11.8%	5.3%	1985	20.3%	5.3%
1936	3.1%	5.3%	1961	1.9%	5.3%	1986	15.1%	5.3%
1937	1.6%	5.3%	1962	5.6%	5.3%	1987	2.9%	5.3%
1938	6.2%	5.3%	1963	1.6%	5.3%	1988	6.1%	5.3%
1939	4.5%	5.3%	1964	4.0%	5.3%	1989	13.3%	5.3%
1940	3.0%	5.3%	1965	1.0%	5.3%	1990	9.7%	5.3%
1941	0.5%	5.3%	1966	4.7%	5.3%	1991	15.5%	5.3%
1942	1.9%	5.3%	1967	1.0%	5.3%	1992	7.2%	5.3%
1943	2.8%	5.3%	1968	4.5%	5.3%	1993	11.2%	5.3%
1944	1.8%	5.3%	1969	-0.7%	5.3%	1994	-5.1%	5.3%
1945	2.2%	5.3%	1970	16.9%	5.3%	1995	16.8%	5.3%
1946	1.0%	5.3%	1971	8.7%	5.3%	1996	2.1%	5.3%
1947	0.9%	5.3%	1972	5.2%	5.3%	1997	8.4%	5.3%
1948	1.9%	5.3%	1973	4.6%	5.3%	1998	10.2%	5.3%
1949	2.3%	5.3%	1974	5.7%	5.3%	1999	-1.8%	5.3%
1950	0.7%	5.3%	1975	7.8%	5.3%	2000	12.6%	5.3%

Source: Calculated by Paul Grangaard using data presented in *Stocks, Bonds, Bills and Inflation® 2001 Yearbook*, ©2001 Ibbotson Associates, Inc. Based on copyrighted works by Ibbotson and Sinquefield. All rights reserved. Used with permission.
Intermediate Term Government Bonds are based on data from The Wall Street Journal and the CRSP Government Bond File. For illustration purposes only. Not representative of an actual investment. Past performance is not a guarantee of future results. An investment cannot be made directly in an index.

fluctuate as much as the stock market, but that their seventy-five-year average annual return is only 5.3 percent. At this lower average annual return, your $10 investment would only have grown to $486 between 1926 and 2000, compared with $25,865 for large company stocks and $64,022 for small company stocks. You would have had a much smoother ride to a much smaller account balance if you had decided to put your money into bonds rather than stocks back in 1926.

Historical Returns as a Guide to "Reasonable" Expectations

You should now have a better understanding of the concept of average annual returns and a better feel for how the markets have actually behaved over the last seventy-five years. Your understanding of long-term historical average annual returns is the starting point in deciding what level of returns to build into your own retirement plan. These historical returns provide a benchmark that you can use to determine the "reasonableness" of the rates of return you choose to use. As always, there are no guarantees of future performance based upon past performance, but you probably shouldn't stray too far from what history has shown to be "reasonable."

7

Time Is Money

Two sides of the same coin in retirement planning are establishing "reasonable" rates of return for your stock market investments and reducing the likelihood that you will earn anything other than those "reasonable" rates. You need to reduce the possibility of getting rates of returns other than what you plan for because you eventually need to create Income Ladders with the growth you expect to earn on your stock market investments. One of the biggest challenges you face as a retirement investor is knowing when and how to harvest that growth.

Using "Reasonable" Rates of Return

You should always use "reasonable" rates of return in your financial plan. Reasonable rates of return have to make sense given the historical long-run averages for the markets you are investing in. Hoping for higher rates of return because they make you feel better doesn't make them any more reasonable. Wishful thinking won't get you very far in retirement. You have to keep your decisions grounded in actual experience—and that means using long-term history as your guide.

Spending the Right Amount in Retirement

During retirement you don't want to spend too much and you don't want to spend too little—you want to spend the right amount. Since you will be basing many of your current and future spending decisions on the long-term rates of return you expect to earn in the stock market, getting more or less than the reasonable rates you are anticipating can cause your plans to go awry. In other words, the possibility of getting rates of return other than the reasonable rates you are building into your plan may cause you to either over- or underspend—which is exactly what you want to guard against. Knowing when to sell stocks to lock in your investment gains is one of the best ways to increase the odds that you will get what you are expecting, and also one of the most important elements of a well-managed retirement plan.

Selling Stock Market Investments

During retirement most people will sell more stock market investments, or equities, than they buy. The term "equities" is just another name for stock market investments—the two terms are interchangeable. During the accumulation phase of life, while you're working and saving for retirement, you generally buy more equities than you sell, and then stay invested to go after the higher rates of return that have historically been available in the stock market. The higher rates of return in the stock market are often what make it possible for many of us to accumulate enough money to retire in the first place. However, once we retire, most of us have to start selling those stocks to create the Income Ladders we need to replace our paychecks.

Buying Stock Market Investments During Retirement

It's not that you will absolutely never buy equities again. There are times in retirement when it makes sense to purchase stocks. Some people do it for fun—because they enjoy trading and managing individual stocks. Others do it because they think it's a good time to reallocate their portfolios for diversification purposes. But usually, when you buy equities during retirement, you are also selling equities too. In other words, you occasionally sell one equity investment to buy another. But in these transactions the total amount invested in the stock market doesn't change—only the mix.

Picking a Time to Sell Stocks During Retirement

Since you are probably going to be an overall seller of equities during retirement, you want to be very careful about when you sell and at what prices. You obviously want to sell when stock prices are up and you certainly don't want to get yourself into a position in which you are forced to sell equities in down markets simply because you are out of cash and need some more money to pay the bills. One of the most important things to understand about retirement investing is that you would always like to be in a position to choose a good time to sell stocks, and never in a position in which you could be forced to sell stocks at the wrong time. This is one of the best ways to protect yourself against the possibility of getting rates of return other than what you are reasonably expecting and building into your plan—because it's only when you sell stocks that you lock in your investment gains and losses.

Stock Market Holding Periods in Retirement

Throughout retirement you will be spending money and managing your lifestyle based in large part on what you think you will earn on your stock market investments. Obviously, if you don't achieve the rates of return you are anticipating, you will probably be spending the wrong amount. So the big question is how to stay invested in the stock market for the growth you may need, while reducing the possibility of getting anything other than what you're expecting—especially when you know that the stock market usually bounces around all over the place from year to year.

One of the answers is stock market holding periods. They are an important part of reducing the likelihood of getting anything other than the "reasonable" rates of return you are building into your plan. Understanding how to use holding periods will change the way you think about investing in general and managing money during retirement in particular, and will impact the way you think and feel about owning stock market investments during retirement.

Stock Market Holding Periods Defined

A stock market holding period is the length of time you can stay invested in the stock market for growth before you have to sell stocks to get the money you need to live on in retirement. In essence, it's the amount of time you have to ride out the ups and downs in the stock market while waiting for the reasonable average annual rates of return you are expecting and building into your plan. Keep in mind that if you get those reasonable rates of return earlier than you expect, you won't necessarily hang on to your equities for the full term of your holding periods. You decide when to sell stocks in retirement—not a preestablished financial plan. Holding periods simply give you a measure of the length of time you can stay invested if you want to, not necessarily the length of time you actually will stay invested. As you will see, holding periods bring flexibility to your plan—not rigidity.

Reasonable Return Expectations: Longer and Shorter Holding Periods

As we have already discussed, long-run historical stock market performance provides a good benchmark for establishing "reasonable" return expectations for planning purposes. But you have to ask—can long-run, seventy-five-year historical average annual rates of return really be used to anticipate what you are likely to earn over much shorter investment periods? The answer is yes and no. Clearly, most of us are not going to live seventy-five years in retirement, and we know that stock market investments will fluctuate on a year-to-year basis. So we have to figure out a way to use long-term historical returns to draw meaningful conclusions about much shorter and more realistic retirement investment periods.

Anticipating Short-Term Stock Market Performance

Is it reasonable to expect an 11 percent average annual rate of return for large company stocks next year just because they produced an 11 percent average annual rate of return over the last seventy-five years? The answer is no. Although it's true that an 11 percent rate of return is probably the best guess you can make about what will happen next year, it's also true that over one-year investment periods it isn't a very good guess. The truth is, long-run average annual returns are a very poor predictor of what might happen in any future one-year period.

A Picture of Short-Term Stock Market Performance

Illustration 19 shows the actual annual returns for every year between 1926 and 2000 for large company stocks. Each dot on the graph represents the rate of return for one year. The shaded line running straight across the graph at 11 percent is the average annual rate of return for the entire seventy-five-year period.

The highest rate of return for any single year was 54 percent in 1933, while the lowest rate was negative 43.3 percent in 1931—and of course the market produced just about everything in between. On a yearly basis, large company stock returns jumped around all over the place, so even though the 11 percent long-run average might be a good estimate for overall planning purposes, it certainly doesn't seem to be a very good predictor of what will happen next year.

One-year investment holding periods are very unpredictable— because the stock market itself is very unpredictable over such short investment horizons. If you think you might need your money in a year or two you would be foolish to put it into the stock market, because it's virtually impossible to predict what

Illustration 19: Annual Large Company Stock Returns
Individual Years (1926 Through 2000)

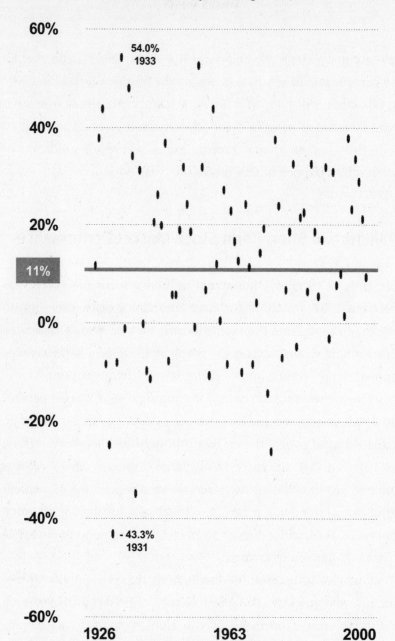

you are likely to get over such short holding periods. It could be very good or it could be very bad—and there is no way to know in advance.

Longer-Term Investment Performance: Five-Year Holding Periods

However, longer holding periods can lead to more predictability. Illustration 20 shows what happens when you consider the average annual rates of return for all five-year holding periods. Although the long-run average annual rate of 11 percent doesn't change—since we are still dealing with the same seventy-five years, the overall range of five-year average annual returns compared to one-year returns changes quite a bit. Not only are the highs and lows much less dramatic, but all of the five-year periods tend to cluster much closer to the 11 percent long-run average—indicating that they are a better "predictor" of what you might actually get over any future five-year period. The best five years, between 1995 and 1999, provided an average annual rate of return of 28.6 percent, while the worst five years, between 1928 and 1932, lost 12.5 percent per year. Obviously, if you are going to plan to get an 11 percent rate of return on your stock market investments, your odds are much better if you can stay invested for at least five years rather than having to sell after just one.

Illustration 20: Average Annual Large Company Stock Returns
Five-Year Holding Periods (1926 Through 2000)

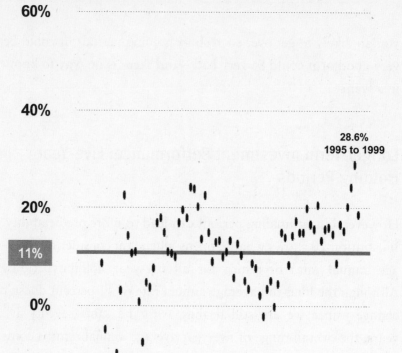

28.6%
1995 to 1999

11%

-12.5%
1928 to 1932

60%

40%

20%

0%

-20%

-40%

-60%

1926   1963   2000

Five-Year Holding Periods: Good but Not Good Enough

The predictive accuracy of the 11 percent long-run average annual return improves a lot as you increase your holding periods from one year to five years. But even with such a big improvement there is still a fairly wide range of returns between the best and the worst five-year period, which can leave some people feeling a little uncomfortable about using the 11 percent long-run average as an estimate in their retirement plan. In other words, if you are going to use long-run historical average annual returns as a basis for determining "reasonable" planning estimates, you may not have a lot of confidence in those estimates if you can only stay invested for five years—because as good as they are, they may not be good enough.

Ten-Year Holding Periods

If five-year holding periods don't give you the confidence you need, how about ten-year holding periods—can they improve the accuracy of the long-run averages you may want to use in your plan? The answer is yes. Illustration 21 shows why. The best average annual rate of return for all ten-year periods was 20.1 percent between 1949 and 1958. The worst ten-year average annual return was negative .9 percent between 1929 and 1938. So the range of returns has come down a lot. In fact, there are

Illustration 21: Average Annual Large Company Stock Returns
Ten-Year Holding Periods (1926 Through 2000)

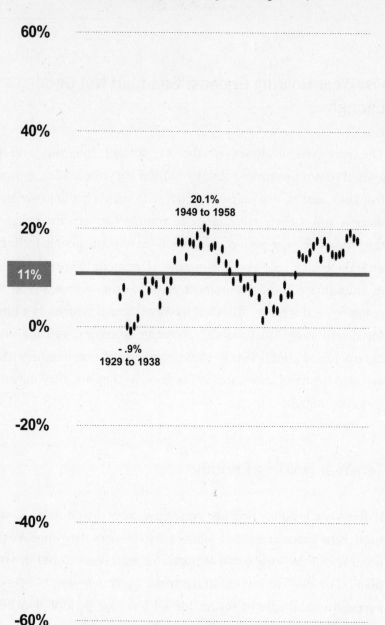

only three ten-year periods in history in which large company stocks lost money. It's also important to notice that over ten-year investment periods all of the returns tend to cluster even more tightly around the long-run average of 11 percent. So the predictive power of the long-run average improves quite a bit as compared to either one- or five-year holding periods.

All the Way Out to Twenty-Year Holding Periods

Illustration 22 shows what happens to investment returns when they are considered over even longer twenty-year holding periods. But you have to remember—unless you are a younger, preretirement investor, it's difficult to have twenty-year holding periods. The definition of a holding period is the length of time you can stay invested in the equities markets for growth before needing to sell stocks to provide income for retirement. The problem is that if you plan to hold stock market investments for twenty years before selling them you will have to wait a long time to harvest any of the growth in your equity accounts. Not only that, but you will also have to use a much larger share of your initial investment resources to provide income for the first twenty years of retirement, which will mean a bigger Income Ladder and less money to invest in historically faster-growing stock market investments. Overall, this can make it much more difficult to accumulate the assets that may be required to provide the inflation-protected income you might need in future years. It's kind of a double whammy, and it generally doesn't work out very well.

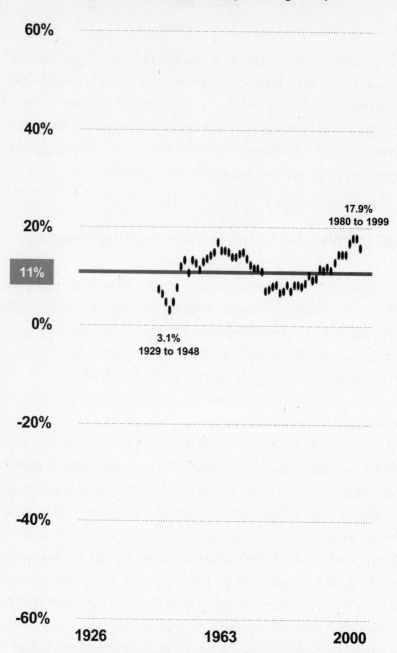

Illustration 22: Average Annual Large Company Stock Returns
Twenty-Year Holding Periods (1926 Through 2000)

60%

40%

20%

17.9%
1980 to 1999

11%

0%

3.1%
1929 to 1948

-20%

-40%

-60%

1926   1963   2000

Nonetheless, there is a modest improvement in the predictive accuracy of the long-run average annual rate of return over twenty-year holding periods. The accuracy is improved because the twenty-year periods in the example tend to cluster a little closer to the long-run average of 11 percent. However, the improvement in the range of returns between the best and worst twenty-year period and the best and worst ten-year period is not that great, and is certainly not as dramatic as it was between one- and five-year holding periods and between five- and ten-year holding periods. So it seems that twenty-year holding periods are a little better than ten-year holding periods, but not much better—and yet they are twice as long!

A Quick Look at Thirty-Year Holding Periods

Illustration 23 shows what happens to the range of returns for all thirty-year holding periods between 1926 and 2000. The best thirty-year period delivered a 13.7 percent average annual rate of return between 1970 and 1999, while the worst thirty-year period delivered an average annual rate of 8.5 percent between 1929 and 1958. The rest of the thirty-year periods cluster very close to the long-run average of 11 percent. So when you consider thirty-year stock market holding periods, the odds of getting anything other than what you are reasonably expecting start to get pretty small.

Illustration 23: Average Annual Large Company Stock Returns
Thirty-Year Holding Periods (1926 Through 2000)

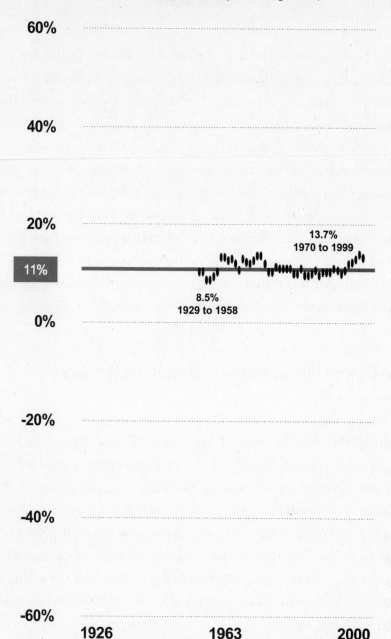

Why Most People Like Longer Holding Periods

What the illustrations make clear is that the longer you can stay invested in the stock market, or in other words, the longer your stock market holding periods, the more likely you are to actually get the long-run historical average annual rates of return that you are reasonably expecting and building into your retirement plan. As a result, you generally want to create the longest possible holding periods during retirement to try to gain as much comfort as possible in your ability to earn the rates of return you are expecting.

You Often Get Less Income with Longer Holding Periods

However, the flip side of the coin is that longer holding periods generally lead to less income during retirement. It works this way because longer holding periods force you to wait longer to sell stocks, and, as a result, you have to keep more money out of the stock market to begin with, because it has to last longer. In other words, you have to create larger initial Income Ladders to take care of your retirement paycheck for longer holding periods. With more money out of the stock market, you will probably get less overall growth. With less overall growth, you will most likely end up with less overall income. It's the double whammy I mentioned a moment ago. So while it's true that you want the longest possible holding periods during retirement, it's also true that you have to balance your need for comfort and predictability in the stock market with the equally important need for reasonable amounts of income.

Reducing Variability with Longer Holding Periods

Illustration 24 shows how longer holding periods tend to reduce the odds of getting rates of return other than what you are expecting. Each of the previous illustrations for one-year, five-year, ten-year, twenty-year, and thirty-year holding periods have been squeezed down into individual bars for comparison purposes. The top and bottom of each bar represent the range of average annual returns for each holding period, and the dots represent the individual holding periods within each bar. As always, the 11 percent long-run average annual rate of return is the same straight line running right across the middle.

As holding periods increase you achieve fairly dramatic reductions in the variability of historical returns around the long-run average. The reduction in variability is very significant as you move from one-year to five-year holding periods and from five-year to ten-year holding periods. But even though you continue to reduce variability as you move beyond ten years, it doesn't really come down much more. This is due to the fact that you can only reduce variability around the long-run average up to a point. You can never get rid of market fluctuations altogether. But you are usually able to squeeze a lot of the variation and unpredictability out of the

Illustration 24: Average Annual Large Company Stock Returns
Various Holding Periods (1926 Through 2000)

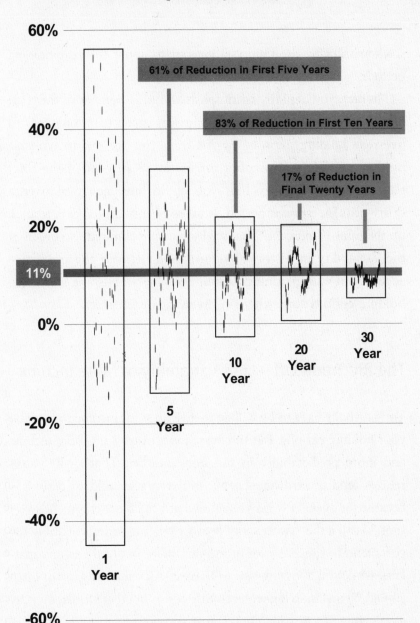

stock market by the time you get out to about ten-year holding periods.

In fact, you actually accomplish about 61 percent of the total historical reduction in variability just by going from one-year to five-year holding periods. By the time you get out to ten-year holding periods you account for about 83 percent of the total reduction in variability that you could have achieved over a thirty-year investment period. It takes twenty more years to pick up the final 17 percent. That's why you can eliminate so much of the variability in historical returns and increase the predictive accuracy of your planning assumptions by establishing and using holding periods somewhere in the range of ten years.

The Big Trade-Off—Less Variability or More Income

You normally have to be willing to give up some income to increase your holding periods. But of course most of us want more income and more predictability in the stock market. That's why many retirees tend toward nine-, ten-, or eleven-year holding periods—because they generally get you into what I call the "retirement sweet spot." I call it the "sweet spot" because holding periods of about ten years tend to squeeze a lot of the variability out of the equity markets, while still allowing you to harvest stock market growth often enough to maintain higher levels of income. In other words, they are long enough to provide the comfort you need concerning the rates of return you are expecting, but not so long that you can't get the income you need to enjoy yourself during retirement.

Limited Reduction in Variability Beyond Ten Years

Another reason people tend not to go much beyond ten-year holding periods is that you get so little reduction in variability as you go from ten- to fifteen-year holding periods—and very little more as you move out to twenty years. So to achieve much of a meaningful reduction in variability beyond ten-year holding periods you have to get out beyond twenty years—and most people can't afford to do that.

Using Ten-Year Holding Periods As a Planning Benchmark

Because of their natural significance, throughout the rest of the book I focus primarily on ten-year holding periods—not because you should always use them, but because they provide a pretty good benchmark. Consequently, it's instructive to consider the average annual rates of return for all sixty-six ten-year holding periods between 1926 and 2000 to see what they can tell us about managing stock market investments during retirement.

Even though there is still some variability in the ten-year average annual rates of return, from a high of 20.1 percent between 1949 and 1958, to a low of minus .9 percent between 1929 and 1938, most of the rates of return throughout all ten-year holding periods tend to cluster fairly close to or in excess of the 11 percent long-run average annual rate.

For example, the upper half of Illustration 25 shows that only 4.6 percent of all sixty-six historical ten-year holding periods had negative ten-year average annual returns. So historically speaking, the chance of losing money in the stock market over ten-year holding periods is pretty small—although of course it is always a possibility.

Slightly over 9 percent of all historical ten-year holding periods delivered average annual rates of return between 0 and 5 percent. Almost 32 percent achieved average annual rates between 5 percent and 10 percent. Over 22 percent delivered rates of return between 10 and 15 percent, and an incredible 31.8 percent, or almost a third of them, actually delivered average annual rates of return of 15 percent or more!

In fact, to get a better perspective on the degree to which rates of return tend to be skewed toward the higher end of the range, the lower half of Illustration 25 summarizes the same data on a cumulative basis. It shows that 31.8 percent of the time large company stocks delivered average annual rates of return greater than 15 percent. It also shows that 54.5 percent of the time you would have earned 10 percent or more if you had the advantage of ten-year holding periods, and that over 86 percent of the time you would have earned at least 5 percent average annual rates of return!

These are important results—because as you know, 5 percent is very close to the seventy-five-year long-run average annual rate of return of 5.3 percent for fixed-income investments like intermediate-term government bonds. So in most instances, over ten-year holding periods, large company stocks have delivered

Illustration 25: Average Annual Large Company Stock Returns
All 66 Ten-Year Holding Periods (1926 Through 2000)

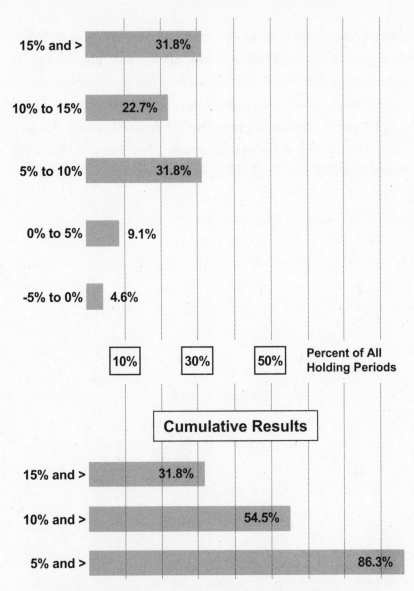

15% and >	31.8%
10% to 15%	22.7%
5% to 10%	31.8%
0% to 5%	9.1%
-5% to 0%	4.6%

10%   30%   50%   **Percent of All Holding Periods**

Cumulative Results

15% and >	31.8%
10% and >	54.5%
5% and >	86.3%

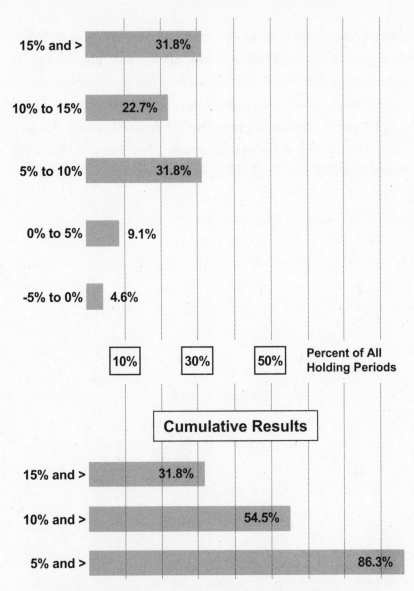

Source: Calculated by Paul Grangaard using data presented in *Stocks, Bonds, Bills and Inflation*® *2001 Yearbook,* © 2001 Ibbotson Associates, Inc. Based on copyrighted works by Ibbotson and Sinquefield. All rights reserved. Used with permission.
Large Company Stocks are based on the S&P Composite Index which includes 500 of the largest stocks in the United States from 1957 to the present and 90 of the largest stocks prior to 1957. For illustration purposes only. Not representative of an actual investment. Past performance is not a guarantee of future results. An investment cannot be made directly in an index.

rates of return very close to or better than their long-run historical average of 11 percent, while almost always providing returns at least as good as or better than the seventy-five-year average annual rate of return for alternative fixed-income type investments. That's why it's not as hard as you may think to follow Principle #6: Be a Long-Term Investor During Retirement, because you can do it pretty well with ten-year holding periods.

8

Living on Growth

Throughout retirement you will need to determine when to sell stock market investments to get the money you need to live on. That's why Principle #7: Know When to Sell is so important. Even though you may create ten-year holding periods for your stock market investments, you won't necessarily hold on to them for the full ten years. In fact, in most instances you will sell them before the end of a typical ten-year period. You do this because as retirement investors you never want to get too close to the point at which you will be forced to sell stocks, because you never know what will be happening in the market at that time.

Like many retirees, you may decide to use ten-year holding periods to increase the odds of earning a reasonable long-run average annual rate of return. Longer holding periods can allow your equity investments to fluctuate up and down over time like they always do, while hopefully settling down to something close to their long-run average. However, after the first year of a ten-year holding period you only have nine years left. After the second year you only have eight years left—and so on, until eventually you have none at all. In other words, year after year you systematically use up your holding periods until eventually you run out of time and are forced to sell stocks to get more income.

But you never want to be forced to sell stocks. So even if you are initially comfortable with ten-year holding periods, by the time you get out to the fifth or sixth year you might start to get a little nervous—because you know you are getting closer to the point at which you will be forced to sell. Therefore, it's usually beneficial to sell before the end of the holding period, take some of your money out of the stock market, set yourself up with some additional income, and push the point at which you will be forced to sell stocks even further out into the future.

Know When to Sell

The problem for retirement investors is establishing criteria to use in deciding when to sell. Having a plan is one thing. Knowing how to use that plan to deal with changing financial circumstances in real time is another thing altogether.

We will consider two strategies for deciding when to sell stocks. One of them has to do with meeting your rate of return objectives and the other has to do with achieving your expected account values.

Hitting Your Rate of Return Objectives

Ten-year holding periods can reduce the possibility of getting rates of return other than what you expect—and they often allow you to do that without having to stay invested for the full ten years—it's just that you can stay invested if you want to. In fact, ten-year holding periods really just set the outside limit on how long you can survive financially without selling stocks, but they do not tell you when to sell—unless of course you wait until the end.

This is very important, because many ten-year holding periods have delivered expected long-run average annual rates of return before the end of ten years. When this happens, as it often does, you need to be prepared to take advantage of the opportunity to sell stocks before you may have planned to.

Hitting Your Expected Account Values

You can also recast the analysis into dollar terms by asking yourself how much money you expect to have at the end of the ten-year period and then just plan to sell whenever you get to that amount. In other words, rather than evaluating whether you achieve your expected rates of return before the end of any given holding period, you consider instead whether or not you hit your anticipated ending value.

What should you do, for example, if you have as much money in your account after five years as you were expecting to have after ten? You would be smart to consider selling—wouldn't you? Of course you would. After all, you would have gotten to your expected value five years ahead of schedule!

Two Ways to Decide When to Sell: Rates of Return and Values

During retirement, if you achieve the results you are expecting ahead of schedule, you will probably decide to sell stocks sooner than you planned. This will help you address some of your future income needs while also making it more comfortable to keep the rest of your money invested in the stock market where it will have a chance to grow at the higher rates of return that have generally been available in equities.

Selling stocks before the end of your holding period can provide two benefits. First, it takes care of some of the income you need for the future so you don't have to worry so much about it later on. And second, it extends your holding periods. In other words, by setting aside more money for future income needs you don't have to worry so much about being forced to sell stock market investments in the near future.

Pulling the Options Together:
A Real Ten-Year Period

Illustration 26 consists of two closely related graphs of an actual ten-year period from 1932 to 1941. It shows how these two strategies can help you decide when to sell stocks. The upper graph relates to the annual rates of return over this period of time. The lightly shaded bars show the expected annual rates of return—which in this example are a slightly conservative 10 percent. The darker bars represent the actual rates of return earned in each of the ten years. As you would expect, they bounced around all over the place between some very good years and some very bad years. This is why you would have used a ten-year holding period in the first place—to give yourself the time you needed to ride out the ups and downs in the market while waiting to achieve an expected long-run average annual rate of about 10 percent.

The black line in the upper graph shows the actual year-to-date average annual rates of return you would have earned by the end of each year. By the end of the second year, the 54 percent actual return in 1933 averaged with the loss of 8.2 percent in 1932 resulted in a two-year average annual rate of return of 18.9 percent. So losing 8.2 percent in the first year followed by a gain of 54 percent in the second year is the same as earning 18.9 percent in each of the two years. As you can see, the year-to-date actual average rates of return fluctuate from year to year as the market delivers its random pattern of ups and downs.

Illustration 26: Deciding When to Sell
Historical Example of Large Company Stocks
for the Period from 1932 to 1941

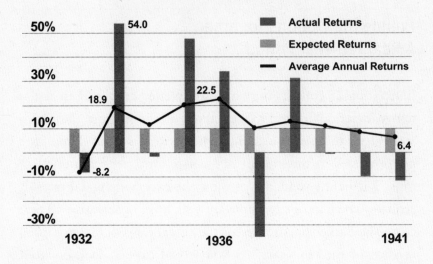

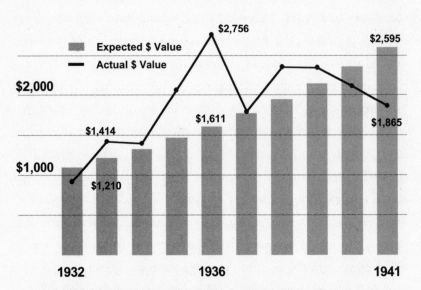

Source: Calculated by Paul Grangaard using data presented in *Stocks, Bonds, Bills and Inflation®* *2001 Yearbook*, © 2001 Ibbotson Associates, Inc. Based on copyrighted works by Ibbotson and Sinquefield. All rights reserved. Used with permission.
Large Company Stocks are based on the S&P Composite Index which includes 90 of the largest stocks prior to 1957. For illustration purposes only. Not representative of an actual investment. Past performance is not a guarantee of future results. An investment cannot be made directly in an index.

The illustration shows that you would have been at or above the expected 10 percent average annual rate of return every year through 1939. In many years you would have been far ahead of expectations. By 1936 you would have earned a 22.5 percent five-year average annual rate of return, which was far better than the 10 percent you were expecting. Obviously, this would have been a great time to consider selling some of your stocks, since you were way ahead of where you thought you would be. In fact, you would have had many opportunities to sell stocks prior to the end of the ten-year period.

Ultimately, however, because of a couple of bad years in 1940 and 1941, the nine- and ten-year average annual rates of return dropped well below your 10 percent expectations. This is why you never want to wait too long to sell stocks—because you never know for sure what might happen next. By waiting until the end of the ten-year period you would actually have gotten quite a bit less than the average annual rate of return you were expecting—even though there were many times throughout the period when you were well ahead of expectations.

Portfolio Values

The lower graph in Illustration 26 relates to the account values over the same ten-year period. The lightly shaded bars show what your account values would have been if you had invested $1,000 at the beginning of 1932 and earned the 10 percent average annual rate of return you were expecting over the entire ten-year period. By 1941 you would have expected your account to have grown to about $2,595. Of course you know it never really happens this way, but it does illustrate what you would have been expecting from an overall planning perspective.

The black line in the lower graph shows the actual value of your investments at the end of each year as they rise and fall with the actual rates of return shown in the upper graph. By the end of the second year, the actual value of your investments was $1,414 compared to an expected value of $1,210. The actual two-year average annual rate of return of 18.9 percent was obviously much better than the average 10 percent rate that you were expecting—and your account value shows it.

By 1936, after having achieved a five-year average annual rate of return of 22.5 percent, your account value would have actually been $2,756, compared to the $1,611 that you would have been expecting after five years. Not only would you have had considerably more value in your account than you planned for, but you would have actually had quite a bit more than the $2,595 that you thought you would have by the end of the entire ten-year period! Would this be a good time to consider selling stocks? Of course it would. Any time you achieve the account values you expect from an entire holding period before the end of that period you need to consider selling—because you never know what will happen next.

In fact, because of the bad years in 1940 and 1941 your account values would have headed south fast, and you would have ended up with a final value of only $1,865—considerably less than the $2,595 that you were expecting. So even though you would have been well ahead of where you thought you would be over most of the ten-year period, by the end of the final year, if you had stayed invested, you would have actually ended up with considerably less than you thought you would. And the problem is that you would almost certainly have been counting on that final value to provide the income you needed to support your lifestyle in future years.

Ten-Year Holding Periods and Selling Stocks Ahead of Schedule

There are normally many opportunities to sell stocks before the end of a typical ten-year holding period—using either an average annual return analysis or an account value analysis. Take a little time to study Illustration 26—you should learn a lot about managing money during retirement.

Although there are never any guarantees about what any future holding period will bring, you should usually be able to find a good opportunity to sell stocks sometime within a typical ten-year holding period. The bottom line is that ten-year holding periods may not only give you a lot of comfort in and of themselves, they may also allow you to enhance that comfort through a well-managed stock sales process. If you know what you're doing, and if you and your advisors spend a little time keeping up with your rates of return and investment values, you should be able to gain a great deal of flexibility, comfort, and control in retirement by making well-timed sales decisions.

9

Dollar-Price-Erosion

The theory is that throughout retirement you should periodically sell equity investments to harvest the growth you hope to earn in the stock market to create Income Ladders to replace your paycheck. However, because the stock market has historically outperformed other investments over time, some people think a better way to do this is to keep more of their money in equities to go after higher rates of return, and then just plan to sell more frequently to get the money they need to live on. In other words, they essentially plan to bypass Income Ladders altogether. This works great if the stock market is always going up. But it can be a disaster when it fluctuates up and down, like it usually does.

Try Not to Sell Stock Market Investments Too Often

Unfortunately, this approach is often recommended by the financial services industry and the financial press. In fact, many investment products actually have built-in features that do it for you—and they may get you into a lot of trouble. Most product literature refers to this process as taking "systematic withdrawals" from your investment accounts, and many financial companies market these features as beneficial product enhancements. I believe that doing it this way is generally a bad idea.

It's important to know when to sell stocks, and it's important to have holding periods that are long enough to give you the time you need to make good sales decisions. But remember, to have longer holding periods you have to build Income Ladders that are big enough to take care of your income needs for reasonably long periods of time.

One of the worst things you can do in retirement is to put too much of your money into the stock market—because it limits your ability to put enough into your Income Ladders. As a result, you may not be able to create the holding periods required to invest successfully in the stock market. By putting too much into equities you may force yourself into selling stocks far more often than you should, and subject yourself to the potentially devastating consequences of dollar-price-erosion.

Investing Too Aggressively

It's important to understand dollar-price-erosion because some people are tempted to invest more aggressively then they should during retirement. By investing too aggressively, I mean owning too much stock. The reason this can be such a big problem is that if you put too much money into the stock market you won't have enough left to create the Income Ladders you need. If you can't create the Income Ladders you need, you won't be able to establish the holding periods you need. If you don't have the holding periods you need, you won't be able to choose appropriate times to sell stock market investments. If you are forced to sell stocks at the wrong time, you may not get the rates of return you are planning for. If you don't get the rates of return you are planning for, you probably won't have enough money to create future Income Ladders—and if you can't create future Income Ladders, you may not be able to maintain the lifestyle you need and want.

Dollar-Price-Erosion in General

For example, in the extreme case, assume you have all of your investments in the stock market. Then, each time you need more money to live on, say at the beginning of each quarter, you will be forced to sell stocks. But selling stocks on a quarterly basis throughout retirement can be extremely dangerous, because you never know what the stock market will be doing when you have to sell. Remember, one of your primary objectives in retirement is to try to make sure that you are never forced to sell stocks at the wrong time. If you have to sell every quarter you are virtually guaranteed that sometimes you will be selling at the wrong time. If this happens too often you can get into big trouble—and it can happen fast. Imagine being forced to sell stock every three months when the market is going down—just to get the money you need to pay your bills, go on vacation, or see the grandkids. It can be very unnerving, and ultimately, very costly.

An Example of Dollar-Price-Erosion

Selling shares too frequently can be very detrimental to older investors who have to sell stocks to get income during retirement. To maintain the same amount of income, you end up having to sell more shares when the market goes down and fewer shares when the market goes up. In other words, you always sell more shares when they are cheap and fewer shares when they are worth more, which is the opposite of what you should do in retirement. Not only that, but you are often forced to sell more shares to get the same amount of income over long retirement periods—and this can be a real problem.

Illustration 27 is made up of two separate but closely related examples. The first is illustrated in columns three through six and the second in columns seven through ten. Together, they show why selling stock market investments too frequently can be such a risky proposition. In both cases we start with $10,000 in the stock market, consisting of 1,000 shares of a large company stock mutual fund valued at $10 per share, and want to generate $739 of inflation-adjusted annual income for a thirty-year retirement period. Keep in mind that mutual funds are an investment that fluctuate with market conditions, and do involve risk—because when redeemed, your shares may be worth more or less than original cost. Mutual funds are available by prospectus only, and you should contact a financial professional or the mutual fund company for a copy of the prospectus. Please read it carefully before investing or sending money.

Inflation-Adjusted Income

Since we want to inflation-protect our lifestyle you will notice in column two that we need more and more income each year. Starting at $739, the amount we need will go up by 3 percent inflation per year—to $761 in year two, to $784 in year three, and so on all the way up to $1,742 in year thirty. As you know, even at an average annual rate of only 3 percent, inflation can have a dramatic effect on our overall need for income over long retirement periods.

Illustration 27: Dollar-Price-Erosion

1	2	3	4	5	6	7	8	9	10
Year	Income Need	Rate of Return	Share Value	Shares Sold	Portfolio Value	Rate of Return	Share Value	Shares Sold	Portfolio Value
0			$10.00	(1,000)	$10,000		$10.00	(1,000)	$10,000
1	$739	10%	$11.00	73.90	$10,187	10%	$11.00	73.90	$10,187
2	$761	10%	$12.10	69.20	$10,369	10%	$12.10	69.20	$10,369
3	$784	10%	$13.31	64.79	$10,543	(10%)	$10.89	64.79	$8,626
4	$808	10%	$14.64	60.67	$10,709	10%	$11.98	74.15	$8,600
5	$832	10%	$16.11	56.81	$10,865	10%	$13.18	69.43	$8,546
6	$857	10%	$17.72	53.19	$11,009	(10%)	$11.86	65.02	$6,920
7	$882	10%	$19.49	49.81	$11,139	10%	$13.05	74.41	$6,641
8	$909	10%	$21.44	46.64	$11,254	10%	$14.35	69.67	$6,306
9	$936	10%	$23.58	43.67	$11,349	(10%)	$12.91	65.24	$4,833
10	$964	10%	$25.94	40.89	$11,423	10%	$14.21	74.66	$4,255
11	$993	10%	$28.53	38.29	$11,473	10%	$15.63	69.91	$3,588
12	$1,023	10%	$31.38	35.85	$11,495	20%	$18.75	65.46	$3,078
13	$1,054	10%	$34.52	33.57	$11,486	10%	$20.63	56.19	$2,227
14	$1,085	10%	$37.97	31.44	$11,441	10%	$22.69	52.61	$1,256
15	$1,118	10%	$41.77	29.44	$11,355	20%	$27.23	49.26	$166
16	$1,151	10%	$45.95	27.56	$11,224	10%	$29.95	42.28	($1,084)
17	$1,186	10%	$50.54	25.81	$11,042	10%	$32.95		
18	$1,221	10%	$55.60	24.17	$10,803	20%	$39.54		
19	$1,258	10%	$61.16	22.63	$10,499	10%	$43.49		
20	$1,296	10%	$67.27	21.19	$10,124	10%	$47.84		
21	$1,335	10%	$74.00	19.84	$9,668	20%	$57.41		
22	$1,375	10%	$81.40	18.58	$9,122	10%	$63.15		
23	$1,416	10%	$89.54	17.39	$8,477	10%	$69.46		
24	$1,458	10%	$98.50	16.29	$7,720	20%	$83.35		
25	$1,502	10%	$108.35	15.25	$6,840	10%	$91.69		
26	$1,547	10%	$119.18	14.28	$5,822	10%	$100.86		
27	$1,594	10%	$131.10	13.37	$4,651	20%	$121.03		
28	$1,642	10%	$144.21	12.52	$3,310	10%	$133.13		
29	$1,691	10%	$158.63	11.72	$1,782	10%	$146.44		
30	$1,742	10%	$174.49	10.98	$0	20%	$175.73		
		10%		1,000		10%		1,000	

Results shown are hypothetical in nature and are not representative of an actual investment. Past performance is not a guarantee of future performance; an investor's results may vary. Mutual funds are an investment that fluctuate with market conditions, and do involve risk. When redeemed, an investor's shares may be worth more or less than original cost. Mutual funds do include fees and expenses which have not been included here in order to simplify the example. If fees and expenses had been included, the results would be lower.

Selling Shares That Are Growing at an Average Annual Rate of Return

In the first example we plan to earn a 10 percent rate of return each year. We know from previous discussions that it's probably reasonable to expect a 10 percent average annual rate of return over a thirty-year investment period, but we would certainly never expect to get 10 percent each and every year. We know that we will do better in some years and worse in others, and that only when we consider the entire period as a whole are we likely to average out to something close to the expected average of 10 percent. However, to illustrate the point we are trying to make, we are going to assume in this first example that we actually get 10 percent each and every year. As a result, the value of our shares in column four increase from $10.00 at the beginning of year one to $11.00 at the end of year one, to $12.10 at the end of year two, to $13.31 at the end of year three, and so on all the way up to $174.49 at the end of year thirty. Keep in mind that this illustration has been simplified and is not representative of an actual investment. Mutual funds include fees and expense which have not been included here in order to simplify the example. If fees and expense had been included, the results would be lower.

Selling Fewer and Fewer Shares Each Year

What happens next? Even though our need for income increases by 3 percent per year, the value of our stock market investments increase even faster—at 10 percent per year. As a result, we can maintain $739 per year of inflation-adjusted income while selling fewer and fewer shares each year. As shown in columns four and five, as the value of our shares increase over time, we are able to sell fewer and fewer of them each year to get the money we need to live on.

By the end of the thirty-year period we will have sold all our shares. So in the example, if we start with 1,000 shares valued at $10 each, and if those shares increase in value at 10 percent per year, for thirty years, with no fluctuations, our $10,000 should be able to provide $739 per year of inflation-adjusted purchasing power for thirty years. We will have achieved our objective. This is the way many software programs and financial planners calculate how you will spend your money during retirement.

Selling Shares That Are Fluctuating in Value

To understand why dollar-price-erosion can be so detrimental, let's turn now to the second example in columns seven through ten. The only difference in assumptions is that we get a little more realistic about the rates of return we expect to earn each year. We know that over thirty years the value, or price, of our stock market investments will jump around all over the place—and we also know that there is no way to predict the actual pattern of future returns. But to make things a little more realistic we'll change the rates of return in every third year, so that we lose 10 percent rather earning 10 percent in years three, six, and nine, and earn 20 percent rather than

10 percent in every third year beyond that. The values shown are simplified for the purposes of illustration, and the actual perform-ance of the market would probably be quite different. But in the illustration, over the entire thirty-year period we will still earn the same 10 percent average annual rate of return—it's just that we start out a little more slowly and then catch up in later years. We start with the same share price of $10.00 and end up with a price of $175.73. This is almost exactly the same as in the first example in which our shares started at $10.00 and grew to $174.49 by earning 10 percent each and every year. In both cases we achieve an average annual rate of return of almost exactly 10 percent.

Selling More Shares to Get the Same Amount of Income Each Year

However, in the second example we have to sell more shares to get the same amount of income each year. Our shares are worth less because of the losses experienced in the early years, so we have to sell more of them to get the same amount of income. For exam-ple, at the beginning of year four we have to sell 74 shares at the previous years ending price of $10.89 each, compared to the first example in which we only had to sell 61 shares at $13.31. Then, in year five, we have to sell 69 shares compared to only 57 in the first example—and so on all the way down to year thirty. In fact, in year twelve we are actually forced to sell almost twice as many shares in the second example as in the first—65 shares instead of only 36, to get the same $1,023 of income.

Running Out of Shares

Ultimately, because we are forced to sell so many more shares each year, by the time we get to year sixteen we actually run out. In fact, we will have sold almost all 1,000 shares by the end of year fifteen, and have only a fraction of the number we need to support ourselves in year sixteen. And of course we won't have any shares left at all to take care of our income needs for the last fourteen years of our life!

And remember, this happens even though we ultimately would have earned a 10 percent average annual rate of return over the entire thirty-year period. But because we have three bad years in the first decade of retirement we end up selling more shares at lower prices throughout the first sixteen years to get the income we need. As a result, by having focused on averages rather than considering that our equity accounts would fluctuate in value over time, we end up selling far more shares each year than we can really afford to sell. And by doing so we don't even have a chance to make it up with the higher 20 percent rates of return we could have earned in later years because we don't have any shares left to earn those higher returns.

The problem is, if you sell shares out of a fluctuating account, and if you start out with a few bad years, you may end up selling so many shares to maintain your income that you run out of stock before you have a chance to catch up. That's why it's so important to keep Principle #8 in mind throughout retirement—Don't Let Dollar-Price-Erosion Catch You Off-Guard. To help protect your-

self, you need holding periods to keep you from having to sell
stock market investments to often.

The Risks Are Simply Too High

That's the negative potential of dollar-price-erosion. Remember, dollar-price-erosion forces you to sell more shares when the
market is down and to sell fewer shares when the market is up—
just to maintain the same level of income. That's the opposite of
what you should do in retirement. You should sell more shares
when the market is up, and fewer or preferable no shares at all
when the market is down.

PART THREE

Flexibility, Comfort, and Control

10

Don't Put All of Your Retirement Eggs into One Basket

Knowing when to sell stocks during retirement is one of the keys to successful retirement investing. The other key is knowing which stocks to sell, because all of your investments may not be doing well at the same time. That's why it's so important to follow Principle #9: Diversify your investments during retirement, because every step of the way you will need to decide which stocks to sell when it's time to harvest some of the growth in your equity accounts. Knowing when to sell and what to sell are what the I call the "twin pillars" of successful stock market investing during retirement.

There Are Different Segments of the Stock Market

There are many different components of what we generally refer to as the "stock market." For analytical purposes the equity markets consist of a variety of different segments that are often referred to as small company stocks, large company stocks, international stocks, growth stocks, value stocks, and a variety of combinations—such as small company growth stocks or large company value stocks.

The reason the market is broken up into these various segments is because each of them tends to perform differently. So while one segment is doing poorly another may be doing better. There can be important benefits for retirement investors who understand this phenomenon and know how to use it to their advantage.

Stock Market Diversification During Retirement

The idea of diversifying during retirement is to spread your equity investments over enough of these different segments of the market to bring the power of average annual returns, holding periods, and stock market sales strategies to a broader range of investments. Even if you don't have a lot of money to spread around you can still diversify by investing in mutual funds that focus on specific market segments.

The big thing during retirement is to attempt to increase the odds that you always have a few equity investments that have achieved their expected overall rates of return, or hit their expected values, by the time you need to sell them to get more income to live on. Diversification during retirement should help you improve the odds that you will always have something in your portfolio that will have done well enough for you to be comfortable selling it. But you do have to keep in mind that diversification, while potentially reducing risk, does not guarantee a profit or protect against a loss.

Deciding What to Sell

When you have a diversified portfolio of stock market investments you should normally be in a position to be able to sell the ones that have done the best. No matter which investments you may have intended to sell when you first created your plan, when it actually comes time to do it you will want to sell the ones that have done the best up until that time.

In other words, even though you may create a ten-year holding period for large company stocks and plan to sell them sometime within those ten years, it's possible that you could run into a period in which you don't actually get the performance you are expecting from these investments. Despite all of the strategies and techniques we have discussed so far this is always a possibility.

That's why it's probably a good idea to invest some of your money in other stock market segments too, like small company stocks or international stocks, which might perform better during the same period of time—and then you could sell them instead. Deciding to own a variety of stock market investments, or in other words, employing stock market diversification during retirement, should make it much easier for you to avoid having to sell any of your stocks at the wrong time.

A Look at Some Enlightening Historical Information

Illustration 28 will help you understand a little more about the performance of various segments of the stock market by showing annual rankings for a number of different categories. Notice that the market as a whole is broken down into seven different segments, each of which is defined by an index used by professional financial managers to chart the performance of the market:

- *large company stocks*, represented by the S&P 500® Index;

- *large company growth stocks*, represented by the S&P 500®/BARRA Growth Index;

- *large company value stocks*, represented by the S&P 500®/BARRA Value Index;

- *small company stocks*, represented by the Russell 2000® Index;

- *small company growth stocks*, represented by the Russell 2000® Growth Index;

- *small company value stocks*, represented by the Russell 2000® Value Index; and

- *foreign stocks*, represented by the MSCI® EAFE® Index.

And finally, *bonds* are represented by the Lehman Brothers Aggregate U.S. Bond Index.

Illustration 28: Annual Winners and Losers in Various Investment Markets (from 1981 to 2000)

Year	Best Performers							Worst Performers
1981	Small Value	Bonds	Small	Large Value	Foreign Stocks	Large	Small Growth	Large Growth
1982	Bonds	Small Value	Small	Large Growth	Large	Large Value	Small Growth	Foreign Stocks
1983	Small Value	Small	Large Value	Foreign Stocks	Large	Small Growth	Large Growth	Bonds
1984	Bonds	Large Value	Foreign Stocks	Large	Large Growth	Small Value	Small	Small Growth
1985	Foreign Stocks	Large Growth	Large	Small	Small Value	Small Growth	Large Value	Bonds
1986	Foreign Stocks	Large Value	Large	Bonds	Large Growth	Small Value	Small	Small Growth
1987	Foreign Stocks	Large Growth	Large	Large Value	Bonds	Small Value	Small	Small Growth
1988	Small Value	Foreign Stocks	Small	Large Value	Small Growth	Large	Large Growth	Bonds
1989	Large Growth	Large	Large Value	Small Growth	Small	Bonds	Small Value	Foreign Stocks
1990	Bonds	Large Growth	Large	Large Value	Small Growth	Small	Small Value	Foreign Stocks
1991	Small Growth	Small	Small Value	Large Growth	Large	Large Value	Bonds	Foreign Stocks
1992	Small Value	Small	Large Value	Small Growth	Large	Bonds	Large Growth	Foreign Stocks
1993	Foreign Stocks	Small Value	Small	Large Value	Small Growth	Large	Bonds	Large Growth
1994	Foreign Stocks	Large Growth	Large	Large Value	Small Value	Small	Small Growth	Bonds
1995	Large Growth	Large	Large Value	Small Growth	Small	Small Value	Bonds	Foreign Stocks
1996	Large Growth	Large	Large Value	Small Value	Small	Small Growth	Foreign Stocks	Bonds
1997	Large Growth	Large	Small Value	Large Value	Small	Small Growth	Bonds	Foreign Stocks
1998	Large Growth	Large	Foreign Stocks	Large Value	Bonds	Small Growth	Small	Small Value
1999	Small Growth	Large Growth	Foreign Stocks	Small	Large	Large Value	Bonds	Small Value
2000	Small Value	Bonds	Large Value	Small	Large	Foreign Stocks	Large Growth	Small Growth

Source: Franklin Templeton Investments. For illustration purposes only. Past performance is not a guarantee of future results. An investment cannot be made directly in an index.

Please remember that an investment can not be made directly in an index. We use this data for informational purposes only. The S&P 500® is an unmanaged index consisting of five-hundred of the most commonly held stocks. The S&P 500®/Barra Growth Index is an unmanaged index generally representative of the U.S. market for growth stocks. The S&P 500®/Barra Value Index is an unmanaged index generally representative of the U.S. market for value stocks. The Russell 2000® Index is an unmanaged index generally representative of the U.S. market for small capitalization stocks. The Russell 2000® Growth Index is an unmanaged index generally representative of the U.S. market for small capitalization stocks. It contains securities that growth managers typically select from the Russell 2000® index. The Russell 2000® Value Index is an unmanaged index generally representative of the U.S. market for small capitalization stocks. It contains securities that value managers typically select from the Russell 2000® index. The MSCI® EAFE® Index tracks the stocks of about 1,000 companies in Europe, Australia, and the Far East (EAFE®). The Lehman Brothers U.S. Aggregate Bond Index tracks investment-grade corporate and government bonds.

Notice that large and small company stocks are broken into separate value and growth components. Value stocks tend to pay higher dividends and often sell at lower prices than comparable companies. They often consist of businesses that are temporarily out of favor with investors and have had their stock prices beaten down to levels that may suggest better "values." Growth stocks on the other hand tend to offer lower dividends because they retain most of their earnings for new business opportunities. They are often growing much faster than the competition and therefore attract more attention and command higher share prices.

There are certainly other ways to break up the stock market for analytical purposes, but don't worry about other categorization schemes or about all the names and acronyms. These are standard categories used by a majority of investment and financial advisors, and we are only using them to make a point. When looking at this kind of information, you should also keep in mind that foreign markets are subject to special risks such as currency fluctuations, political instability, differing securities regulations and periods of illiquidity.

Twenty Years' Worth of Experience to Rely On

Twenty years is long enough to give you a feel for the importance of diversification. As you go from left to right across the chart, you move from the best performing segment of the stock market to the worst performing segment of the market. In most years the differences between the rates of return of the best performers and the rates of return of the worst performers are substantial.

For example, in 1992, small company value stocks, the best performing segment of the market that year, returned approximately 29 percent, while foreign stocks, the worst performing segment of the market, lost over 12 percent. All of the other segments of the market were somewhere in between. By contrast, in 1998, large company growth stocks returned about 42 percent as the best performing segment of the market, while small company value stocks lost about 6.5 percent as the worst performing segment.

Market Leadership Changes from Year to Year

Since you never know which segments of the market will be doing better in any given year, and because you would always like to have at least one or two segments in your stock portfolio in a good position to sell when you need more income, you should try to own a diversified portfolio of all these different types of investments during retirement.

What Really Makes Diversification So Great?

Imagine that during retirement you own a diversified portfolio of equity investments covering all seven categories of the market. To keep it simple, assume that you spread your equity investments equally across all of the different market segments by purchasing a different mutual fund for each category. Further, imagine that you create ten-year holding periods for all of your stock market investments.

Then, think about the whole issue of deciding when to sell equities. Consider all of the tools and techniques you have at your disposal. Imagine being able to compare year-to-date rates of return and account values against your plan for all seven market segments. Imagine being able to decide not only when to sell stocks, but which of the seven categories to sell. Just think about all the opportunities you would have to sell before the end of your holding periods if you had seven different equity investments bouncing around toward their long-run average annual rates of return, with you and your advisors constantly on the lookout for a good time to sell.

We don't have the space in this book to analyze all of the data concerning holding periods and average annual returns for each market segment like we did for large company stocks—but essentially they all work the same. Of course you always need to determine appropriate rates of return and holding periods for the segments of the market in which you plan to invest, but using longer holding periods to reduce the possibility of getting anything other than the reasonable rates of return you build into your plan generally works the same way for each of them.

For example, whereas large company stocks returned 11 percent per year between 1926 and 2000, small company stocks returned about 12.4 percent. So you should probably expect higher average annual rates of return from your small company stock investments than you do from your large company stock investments. Your advisors can help you make these determinations based upon actual historical data much like we have been using for large company stocks.

Additionally, you have already seen that small company stocks tend to fluctuate more in value from year to year than large company stocks, and therefore may tend to take a little longer to average out to their long-run historical performance. That's why you may want to use slightly longer holding periods for small company stocks than for large company stocks.

At any rate, once you decide on the rates of return and holding periods for each segment of the market in which you plan to invest, the overall process of using historical average annual rates of return, reasonable-length holding periods, and intelligent stock market sales strategies come together in a way that should help you achieve your overall retirement planning objectives.

11

Don't Pay Uncle Sam Before You Have To

Although this is not a book about income and estate taxes you do need to work with your accounting, tax, and financial advisors to integrate these important considerations into your plan. Special rules and regulations surrounding the use of IRAs, qualified retirement plans, annuities, trusts, and taxable investments during retirement will complicate your tax situation significantly. You must get professional help in these areas.

The primary concern with taxes in this book is to explain in a very general way how the overall process of managing money during retirement can be negatively affected by taxes, and the potential impact they can have on your retirement income.

Selling Stocks and Creating Income Ladders

Creating and spending Income Ladders over reasonably long holding periods should hopefully give your stock market investments a chance to grow at the higher rates of return you may need to be able to create future Income Ladders and future holding periods. This process will probably repeat itself many times throughout a typical thirty-year retirement period, which means that in most cases you will be making a large number of stock sales during retirement. The issue we need to address from a tax perspective is the exposure you may have to paying income and/or capital gains taxes, or what I call "liquidity taxes," every time you sell stocks to purchase Income Ladder investments.

"Liquidity Taxes"

I call them "liquidity taxes" because you usually have to pay them when you sell stocks to get "more liquid" in your retirement portfolio—or in other words, when you sell stocks to get more income to live on. As you attempt to replace the income you had before you retired, you periodically move money out of the stock market and into Income Ladder investments that are structured to provide the income you want, when you want it. The good thing about using Income Ladders is that they make it possible for you to do this well in advance of when you actually need the money.

However, if you have to pay "liquidity taxes" every time you sell stock market investments to create Income Ladders, you might not be able to achieve the level of income or liquidity you need, because you may not be able to afford to pay all of these taxes up front. You don't want to be forced to pay income and/or capital gains taxes too soon just because you want to move some money into "more liquid" investments. You almost always have to pay taxes when you take money out of your Income Ladders, but that's a very different matter than having to pay them up front just because you want to convert some stocks into Income Ladders in anticipation of future income needs.

Investing in Tax-Deferred Accounts

If you already have your money in tax-deferred accounts like IRAs, retirement plans, variable annuities, and certain kinds of trusts, you don't have to worry about this "liquidity tax" issue. In each of these kinds of accounts you don't have to pay income taxes until you actually take the money out of your Income Ladders. In other words, you can buy and sell investments without paying taxes as long as you don't take the money out of the account. If you just move it around, like you do when you sell stock market investments to create an Income Ladder, you don't have to pay any taxes at the time of the transaction because you only pay taxes when you take the money out and spend it. This can make a big difference in the amount of income you will be able to generate over long retirement periods. Since we are talking about annuities again, it is important to remember that an investment in a variable annuity does involve investment risk, including possible loss of principal. Annuities are designed for long-term retirement investing, and withdrawals of taxable amounts are subject to income tax and, if taken prior to age fifty-nine-and-a-half, a 10 percent federal tax penalty may apply. Early withdrawals may also be subject to withdrawal charges, and annuity contracts, when redeemed, may be worth more or less than the total amount invested. Withdrawals from IRA's and retirement plans are also subject to income tax, and if taken prior to age fifty-nine-and-a-half, a 10 percent federal tax penalty may also apply.

Investing in Taxable Accounts

If you have some of your money in taxable accounts you will probably have to pay annual income taxes on some of the earnings while also paying taxes on the rest of the earnings at the time you sell your investments to create Income Ladders. In taxable accounts, if you haven't paid income taxes on all of your earnings by the time you sell stocks to purchase Income Ladder investments you will most likely have to pay the rest of the taxes at that time. In other words, you incur a "liquidity tax." You are forced to pay taxes simply because you want to restructure your portfolio to include more fixed-income investments.

As a result, you may end up paying taxes much sooner than you would if you were in a tax-deferred account—because in tax-deferred accounts you don't have to pay annual income taxes or "liquidity taxes." In tax-deferred accounts you only pay taxes when you take money out of your Income Ladders—which, as you know, takes place over many years. In essence, you are able to defer the payment of income taxes on your investment gains, allowing you to keep that extra money invested in the stock market where it has a chance to grow at potentially higher rates of return.

Missing Out on Potential Compounded Growth

In taxable accounts you generally pay taxes sooner than you would otherwise have to, and you miss out on the opportunity to keep those unpaid taxes invested in the stock market. Think about the potential compounding you give up. Think about the assets you could leave in the stock market, going after higher rates of return, and compounding on a tax-deferred basis, if you have your investments in tax-deferred accounts. It can amount to a lot of money! And of course all that extra money could be used to generate more income and a better lifestyle.

More Income from Tax-Deferred Accounts

In many cases you are able to generate more income from the same amount of assets if they are invested in tax-deferred accounts like IRAs, retirement plans, and annuities than if you leave them in taxable accounts. That's why as a retiree you need to talk with financial professionals about the merits of getting your taxable investments into tax-deferred vehicles.

Of course this is not always the best answer—depending upon your overall financial and estate planning objectives. There are reasons you may want to leave some of your assets in taxable accounts—but you want to make sure you know what they are. Otherwise, you might be giving up retirement income that you can't afford to give up without even knowing it.

Taxable Accounts in Retirement

Any investments you already have in retirement plans at work, in regular or Roth IRAs, or in annuities or certain kinds of trusts are already in tax-deferred accounts. So you generally don't need to do anything special with them from a tax perspective.

However, most people tend to get to retirement with a lot of taxable investments too. They save and invest in taxable accounts over the years, perhaps sell a home or other investments, and maybe even sell a business. Many people also receive gifts and inheritances. So for a lot of reasons you may get to retirement with substantial amounts of money in taxable investments. You need to take a very hard look at these assets to determine whether or not you should move them into tax-deferred accounts.

You may wonder about getting potentially larger amounts of money into tax-deferred vehicles. Most people know that there are significant limitations on how much you can put into IRAs each year, and since you will be retired you won't be able to use your retirement plans at work either. This only leaves a couple of options. You can use some of the annuity products we've talked about—including single-premium immediate annuities, fixed annuities and variable annuities, or you can use certain kinds of trusts. Many of them have no limitations on how much can be invested at any given time, so it's usually fairly easy to move money into them whenever you want to.

Which kind of account or product to use and whether or not to make the move in the first place are issues you have to take up with your advisors—but you certainly don't want to leave the opportunities unexamined. Ultimately, these decisions can make a big difference in how much income you can get out of your retirement portfolio for the rest of your life.

Rethinking Annuities

In fact, many people need to change the way they think about some of these financial products—if they ever thought about them in the first place. A lot of people have grown up with the idea that annuities are only good to accumulate money for retirement. This is generally not the case. It's certainly true that they continue to be one of the best and most useful accumulation tools you have as a preretirement investor. But you should also recognize the tremendous value of the tax deferral characteristics of annuities during retirement too.

In fact, the idea that annuities, and tax deferral in general, are only important before retirement, seems to come right out of the same kind of thinking that suggests that you should get very conservative with your investments during retirement. These ideas may have been reasonable in the past, but they don't seem to hold water today. In the twenty-first century you will probably need tax deferral as much during retirement as you ever did before retirement.

Tax Deferral Before and During Retirement

These days you have to be smarter. You have to understand how important it may be to manage your portfolio in tax-deferred accounts during retirement. You need to learn how to protect your assets and income from "liquidity taxes," and you need to understand that annuities are not just for accumulating assets for retirement. They can also play a fundamental, unique, and important role during retirement too—so much so that many people may actually purchase them for the first time in retirement.

Again, you need to talk with financial professionals about these matters. There are many issues surrounding when and how to use annuities—both before and during retirement, and there are numerous varieties and options to choose from. But you will often find yourself able to generate more income from the same amount of assets if you decide to invest in tax-deferred rather than taxable accounts.

Illustration 29: Liquidity Tax Analysis

Year	Taxed Annually		Taxed at End of 10-Year Periods		Taxed at End of 10-Year Periods with Tax Paid Over Following 10 Years	
	Ending Balance	Annual Tax Amount	Ending Balance	Annual Tax Amount	Ending Balance	Annual Tax Amount
0	$1,000		$1,000		$1,000	
1	$1,070	$30	$1,100	$0	$1,100	$0
2	$1,145	$32	$1,210	$0	$1,210	$0
3	$1,225	$34	$1,331	$0	$1,331	$0
4	$1,311	$37	$1,464	$0	$1,464	$0
5	$1,403	$39	$1,611	$0	$1,611	$0
6	$1,501	$42	$1,772	$0	$1,772	$0
7	$1,606	$45	$1,949	$0	$1,949	$0
8	$1,718	$48	$2,144	$0	$2,144	$0
9	$1,838	$52	$2,358	$0	$2,358	$0
10	$1,967	$55	$2,116	$478	$2,594	$0
11	$2,105	$59	$2,327	$0	$2,805	$48
12	$2,252	$63	$2,560	$0	$3,038	$48
13	$2,410	$68	$2,816	$0	$3,294	$48
14	$2,579	$72	$3,097	$0	$3,576	$48
15	$2,759	$77	$3,407	$0	$3,885	$48
16	$2,952	$83	$3,748	$0	$4,226	$48
17	$3,159	$89	$4,123	$0	$4,601	$48
18	$3,380	$95	$4,535	$0	$5,013	$48
19	$3,617	$101	$4,989	$0	$5,467	$48
20	$3,870	$108	$4,476	$1,012	$5,965	$48
21	$4,141	$116	$4,923	$0	$6,447	$115
22	$4,430	$124	$5,416	$0	$6,976	$115
23	$4,741	$133	$5,957	$0	$7,558	$115
24	$5,072	$142	$6,553	$0	$8,198	$115
25	$5,427	$152	$7,208	$0	$8,902	$115
26	$5,807	$163	$7,929	$0	$9,677	$115
27	$6,214	$174	$8,722	$0	$10,529	$115
28	$6,649	$186	$9,594	$0	$11,467	$115
29	$7,114	$199	$10,554	$0	$12,498	$115
30	$7,612	$213	$9,469	$2,140	$13,632	$115

For illustration purposes only. Not representative of an actual investment.

Different Ways of Being Taxed in Retirement

Illustration 29 should give you a better feel for the consequences of paying income taxes too soon in retirement. It shows three different methods of taxing the growth in a portfolio. In each case you start with $1,000, assume that it grows at 10 percent per year for thirty years, and that you pay a combined state and federal income tax rate of 30 percent. However, in each example, you will pay the tax differently.

Keep in mind that these are very simple examples and don't take into account many of the complexities concerning the way investment earnings are actually taxed. They are only intended to show in a very general way the consequences of paying income taxes at different times during retirement.

Tax Example One—Growth Taxed Annually

If you assume that you invest in a taxable account and pay taxes on all of your investment earnings each year, a $1,000 investment will grow to about $7,612 over thirty years. You earn 10 percent each year on the cumulative balance and pay 30 percent of those earnings in taxes every year. So in year one your $1,000 investment earns $100, you pay $30 in taxes, and you end the year with $1,070 in your account.

By the time you get to year ten, you start with $1,838 in your account, earn $181, pay $52 in taxes, and end the year with

$1,967. The process continues the same way until by the end of the thirty-year investment period you have $7,612 in the account.

Tax Example Two — Growth Taxed at the End of Each Ten-Year Period

If you assume that you invest in a taxable account, but that you don't have to pay taxes on your investment earnings until the end of each ten-year period, the outcome is very different. The second example shows what happens if you only have to pay taxes every ten years—much like when you sell stocks to create Income Ladders. In other words, it assumes that all of your taxes are paid like "liquidity taxes" would be paid.

In this case, by the end of the thirty-year period you have about $9,469 in your account—$1,857 more than in the first example. In other words, you accumulate about 24 percent more because you pay the taxes later and are therefore able to leave the money invested longer.

In this case, your $1,000 compounds at 10 percent each year with no taxes taken out until the end of each ten-year period. Instead of paying taxes every year, you only pay them three times over the entire thirty-year period—and each time, you pay all the taxes that are due on the previous ten years' earnings. Ultimately, even though you are paying a "liquidity tax" every ten years, you still accumulate substantially more money this way.

Tax Example Three—Growth Taxed at the End of Each Ten-Year Period with the Tax Paid Over the Following Ten Years

Now, let's assume that you invest in a tax-deferred account so you don't have to pay the "liquidity tax" all at once at the end of each ten-year period. Instead, let's assume that you are able to spread it out over the following ten years like you would if you only had to pay tax when you took money out of an Income Ladder. In other words, you compute the tax at the end of each ten-year period, but pay it in equal annual installments over the following ten years. Of course this means that all those taxes you're not paying will be able to stay invested even longer—and the results are significant.

Over the thirty-year period you will end up with $13,632 in the account. That's $4,163 more than the second example and $6,020 more than the first example. By paying the tax in equal annual installments over the ten years following each ten-year period you end up with substantially more in the account at the end of thirty years.

These are the kinds of differences you have to consider when you decide how to invest your taxable assets. This is the potential value of deferring both the annual taxes and the "liquidity tax" payments. Illustration 30 shows graphically just how dramatic the differences can be. With this level of tax deferral you should be able to earn additional returns on all of the taxes that you don't have to pay along the way. In total, it can add up to some significant amounts of money.

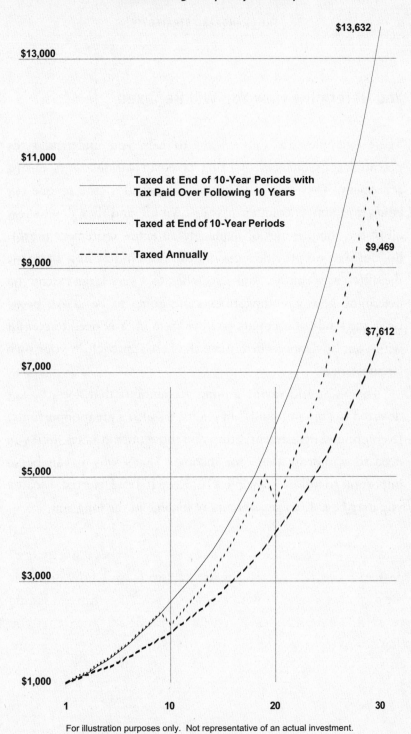

Illustration 30: Liquidity Tax Graph

$13,632

$13,000

$11,000

——— Taxed at End of 10-Year Periods with
Tax Paid Over Following 10 Years

·········· Taxed at End of 10-Year Periods

- - - - - Taxed Annually

$9,000

$9,469

$7,612

$7,000

$5,000

$3,000

$1,000

1   10   20   30

For illustration purposes only. Not representative of an actual investment.

You Determine How You Will Be Taxed

These examples are only meant to help you understand the potential consequences of being taxed in various ways during retirement. They don't take into account all of the unique tax issues you may encounter in your own life and they don't show all of the complexities of managing an entire retirement portfolio. But they do provide a good illustration of just how dramatic the differences can be. And remember, to a very large extent you determine how your investments are going to be taxed, based upon the kinds of accounts you put them in. You need to consult with your advisors to determine the best approach in your own circumstances.

There's an old saying among accountants that goes, "a tax deferred is a tax not paid." In reality, it's also a great opportunity to compound investment returns on those unpaid taxes until you need to withdraw them for income. That's why it can be so important to follow Principle #10: Keep It Tax Deferred, because you may be able to generate more income in the long run.

Invest Right During Retirement

In the following chapter we provide some examples and work-sheets to help you get started on your own plan. But before we do that let's take a quick look at the inner workings of a sample portfolio that uses the Grangaard Strategy™ and compare it to a couple of others that don't.

The following three examples use different assumptions and variables to reflect the different ways you might actually manage your money during retirement. While looking at these examples, keep in mind that you ultimately have to decide for yourself which method and/or assumptions make the most sense in your own circumstances—but no matter what strategy you decide to use, you have to follow Principle #11: Have a Plan.

Using the Grangaard Strategy™

In the first example we put the Grangaard Strategy™ into action. It will allow us to pull together all of the concepts and ideas we have been talking about throughout the book.

Let's start with a summary of the key variables. First, we assume that you bring $739,129 with you into retirement—and that you have it in a rollover IRA. That's the amount of money we ended up with in Chapter 5: Keep Your Kettle Full by investing $100 per month for forty years and earning an 11 percent rate of return inside a company retirement plan. Since you're in an IRA we can assume that you will be able to manage the money inside a tax-deferred account throughout retirement.

Next, we assume that you want to provide inflation-protected retirement income for thirty years at a 3 percent inflation rate, and that you want to get your income on a quarterly basis.

As for rates of return—we assume 5 percent interest on your Income Ladder investments, 10 percent average annual rates of return on your large company stock investments, and 12 percent average annual rates of return on your small company stock investments.

Starting With Ten-Year Holding Periods

In the first example we use ten-year stock market holding periods for all of your equity investments. In reality, you will probably use slightly longer holding periods for small company stocks because they tend to fluctuate more in value. However, to keep it simple for illustration purposes we assume ten-year holding periods on all stock market investments.

Portfolio Allocations

You and your advisors ultimately have to decide how to allocate your resources between Income Ladder investments and stock market investments. There are an infinite number of possibilities, but we are going to use an allocation that makes sense from a general historical perspective, knowing that there are no one-size-fits-all solutions to any of our planning decisions. After due consideration, we decide to put 50 percent of your initial investment capital into the first Income Ladder and to split the remaining 50 percent evenly between large company stocks and small company stocks. As you will see, things work out quite well this way.

Summary of Assumptions

So we assume all of the following:

- a thirty-year retirement period;

- quarterly income payments;

- a 3 percent inflation rate;

- ten-year stock market holding periods;

- 5 percent interest on Income Ladder investments;

- 10 percent rates of return on large company stocks;

- 12 percent rates of return on small company stocks; and

- an initial portfolio allocation of 50 percent Income Ladder investments and 50 percent stock market investments— split evenly between large company and small company stocks.

That's it—we're ready to go.

Overall Income and Capital Values

The two graphs in Illustration 31 show what happens to the total value of the portfolio and the amount of income you can take out of it for thirty years. The upper graph shows that your beginning capital of $739,129 grows by more than $1 million dollars to over $1,785,000 by the end of thirty years. This should not come as a surprise given our earlier discussions about how well-managed retirement portfolios tend to maintain their value over time. In fact, the real value of the initial $739,129 remains virtually unchanged over the thirty-year period, since the final amount of $1,785,209 is worth about $735,000 in today's purchasing power.

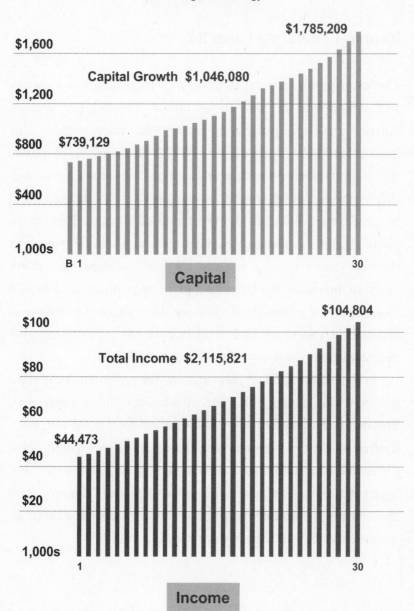

Illustration 31: 30-Year Retirement Portfolio
Capital and Income Values
The Grangaard Strategy™

$1,785,209

$1,600

Capital Growth $1,046,080

$1,200

$800 **$739,129**

$400

1,000s

B 1   30

Capital

$104,804

$100

Total Income $2,115,821

$80

$60

$44,473

$40

$20

1,000s

1   30

Income

For illustration purposes only. Not representative of an actual investment.
Past performance is not a guarantee of future results.

Income-Generating Capacity

The lower graph shows that while your total capital is growing, you should also be able to get about $44,473 per year of inflation-protected purchasing power for thirty years. This means that you will get about $44,473 of income in year one, that it should increase each year at a 3 percent inflation rate, and that by the end of retirement, in year thirty, the portfolio should be generating about $104,804 of annual income. Remember, although this is substantially more than you will be getting in the first year, it's really just the amount you need after thirty years to maintain the original purchasing power of $44,473 based upon the assumed inflation rate. Overall, the portfolio will generate in excess of $2.1 million over the entire thirty-year period without using any of your original capital!

In the example, all of your income during retirement is coming from the earnings on your investments during retirement. You will not use any of your initial capital for income purposes. It often works this way—as remarkable as it may seem. It's also the reason why good financial planning should lead to estate and legacy planning—because with good financial planning you should be in a position where you will need to decide what to do with the money you have left at the end of your life.

Illustration 32: 30-Year Retirement Portfolio
The Grangaard Strategy™

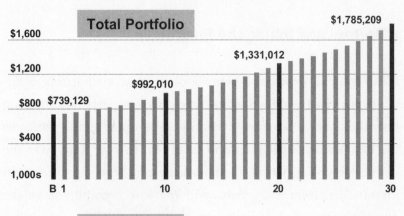

Total Portfolio

- $1,785,209
- $1,331,012
- $992,010
- $739,129

$1,600
$1,200
$800
$400
1,000s

B 1   10   20   30

Stock Market

- $1,611,991
- $1,199,473
- $892,521
- $369,564

$1,600
$1,200
$800
$400
1,000s

B 1   10   20   30

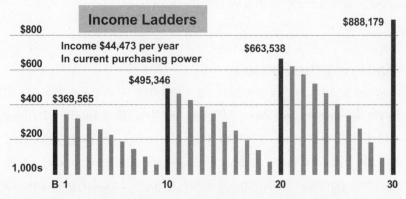

Income Ladders

Income $44,473 per year
In current purchasing power

- $888,179
- $663,538
- $495,346
- $369,565

$800
$600
$400
$200
1,000s

B 1   10   20   30

For illustration purposes only. Not representative of an actual investment.
Past performance is not a guarantee of future results.

A Better Look Inside the Portfolio

Illustration 32 provides a better look at how this portfolio actually works by breaking it into three different parts and showing how they evolve together over time. The upper graph indicates the total value of the portfolio on a year-to-year basis over the entire thirty-year period; the middle graph shows the amount in the stock market each year; and the lower graph shows the amount in Income Ladder investments.

By comparing these three graphs over time you can get a pretty good overview of the process that goes on inside a well-managed portfolio throughout a typical thirty-year retirement period. Many people are surprised at how the total value of the portfolio increases over time in the upper graph as you spend money out of your Income Ladders. The reason it works this way is because the portfolio is designed to replace the principal and interest you are spending out of your Income Ladders with the growth you are expecting in the stock market.

Managing the Portfolio

In the example, you put $369,565 into the first Income Ladder and leave the other $369,564 in the stock market, allocated equally between large company and small company stocks. Over the first ten years you spend your Income Ladder investments down to zero while your stock market investments are designed to grow at historically higher rates of return. Then, at the end of the tenth year, you sell some of the stock market investments to purchase new Income Ladder investments. You might purchase treasury bonds, bank CDs, single-premium immediate annuities, or any of a variety of other fixed-income investments. The bottom line, however, is that at the end of ten years—and at the end of each subsequent ten-year period, you sell some of your equity investments to get the money you need to create the next Income Ladder. If you are considering using CDs, keep in mind that they are FDIC insured up to $100,000 and offer a fixed rate of return. The FDIC insurance applies in the case of bank insolvency, but it does not protect market value. The other investments we talk about are not insured and their principal and yield may fluctuate with market conditions.

The Total Value of the Portfolio

As you can see, over the course of the entire thirty-year period the total dollar amount of the portfolio in our example is likely to increase. It works this way because each Income Ladder you create has to be larger than the previous one to provide the increasing amounts of inflation-adjusted income you need each year. Consequently your equity investments also have to grow larger during each holding period to fund these bigger and bigger Income Ladders. The result of all that growth in the stock market is that you often have a fair amount of money left in your account at the end of your life.

Illustration 33: 30-Year Retirement Portfolio
The Grangaard Strategy™ with 5-Year Stock Sales

Total Portfolio

$1,600

$1,200 $1,208 $1,294

$800 $739 $826 $919 $1,015 $1,112

$400

1,000s
B 1   5   10   15   20   25   30

Stock Market

$1,600

$1,200 $1,138

$800 $630 $730 $847 $981

$400 $369 $543

1,000s
B 1   5   10   15   20   25   30

Income Ladders

$800

Income $44,473 per year
In current purchasing power

$600

$400 $369 $398 $422 $439 $445 $434 $397

$200

1,000s
B 1   5   10   15   20   25   30

For illustration purposes only. Not representative of an actual investment.
Past performance is not a guarantee of future results.

Testing the Portfolio with Five-Year Stock Sales

Illustration 33 shows what happens if you decide to sell stocks every five years rather than every ten years. You often do it this way to minimize the likelihood that you will be forced to sell equities at the wrong time. Once you create your retirement plan you should always evaluate its viability assuming more frequent stock sales. The example assumes that everything remains the same as the original portfolio except that you plan to sell stocks every five years instead of every ten years. The question is, can you maintain the same amount of income?

Overall Income Amounts Using Five-Year Stock Sales

And in fact you can—even if you sell stocks more often. In this example, you can provide the same $44,473 of annual purchasing power as in the original example. So from an income standpoint you should be safe if you ultimately decide to sell stocks every five years rather than every ten years. In both cases you should be able to generate total retirement income of $2,115,821—virtually every dollar you need to support your lifestyle for thirty years.

But You End Up with Less Ending Capital

But there is usually a cost associated with selling stocks more frequently. And that cost generally shows up as a reduction in the total amount of capital you have left at the end of your life. You have to face the question of how much growth you are willing to give up in your stock market investments in order to be able to sell them more frequently to replenish your Income Ladders more often.

If you decide to sell stocks more frequently, the overall effect is to level out the amount of money you have in your Income Ladders and to reduce the amount you have in the stock market. If you sell stocks more often, you take money out of the stock market more frequently, and therefore have less invested to grow at the higher rates of return generally available in the stock market. At the same time, however, you also reduce the dramatic fluctuations in the amount of money you have invested in your Income Ladders. Rather than waiting until the money is almost gone, you actually replenish your Ladders more often than you need to, which means that you maintain a much larger and more consistent balance. This may be very comforting when you're retired because it's generally beneficial to have more "income-ready" assets outside of the stock market—available if and when you need them.

The downside of doing it this way is that you will most likely have less in your account at the end of your life. With more money in Income Ladder investments and less in the stock market you generally earn a lower combined rate of return and therefore probably won't accumulate as much—which may or may not be a concern, depending upon your wealth transfer and legacy plans.

In the example, the total growth in your portfolio has, in fact, almost been cut in half. You are left with total capital of $1,294,326 at the end of thirty years. In other words, you only get about half as much growth in your portfolio as you did by selling stocks every ten years. But still, I believe most people would agree that if you can get to the end of retirement with $1,294,326 left in your account, while generating all of the income you need for thirty years, you will probably be more than satisfied with the results.

More Overall Comfort with the Original Plan

For most people this simply wouldn't be a problem—and it's just kind of a theoretical issue anyway, because you really don't know what you're going to do until you actually do it. You don't know if you are going to sell stocks in four years, six years, eight years, or ten years. But the analysis shows that you can probably be comfortable with your plan whenever you ultimately decide to sell. You know that it should work if you hang on to your stocks for longer holding periods and you know that it should work if you hang on to your stocks for shorter holding periods. In other words, you have a plan that affords you a great deal of flexibility in the face of changing market conditions.

If you sell stocks every ten years you may end up with more money at the end of your life—but you may also have to hold on to your stocks until the end of every holding period. This may cause a fair amount of discomfort in the last two or three years of each ten-year period because you know the time is coming when you will be forced to sell stocks—and of course you won't have any idea about what the markets will be doing at that time.

That's why it's always helpful to see if you can meet your income objectives while selling stocks sooner—because you probably will if you can. But you may also have to be willing to give up a little capital at the end of your life—which is not a big deal for most of us.

Creating "Deferred" Income Ladders

If you have enough in your Income Ladders to last until the end of your holding periods, what do you do with the money when you decide to sell stocks sooner than you planned? It's really no big deal. When you get to a point where it makes sense to sell stocks, you just go ahead and do it. Then, you use the proceeds to create a "deferred" Income Ladder. A "deferred" Income Ladder is just like a regular Income Ladder except that it doesn't start providing income until a future point in time. In other words, the income flow is "deferred" into the future. This allows you to get your money out of the stock market when it makes sense to do so without having to start using it for income right away. After all, you probably still have plenty of money left in your original Income Ladder if you're selling stocks before the end of a holding period. So you simply finish spending the original Income Ladder and then dip into the new "deferred" Income Ladder as necessary.

For example, let's say you are six years into a ten-year holding period and decide to sell some stocks because you've reached your investment objectives ahead of schedule. You don't need any more income because you probably still have enough set aside in your first Income Ladder to carry you through the next four years.

Since you don't need the income right away, you create a "deferred" Income Ladder by putting the proceeds of the stock sale into a fixed annuity contract for the remaining four years. Then, four years from now, you convert the fixed annuity into a single-premium immediate annuity. These kinds of conversions may be achieved through the 1035 exchanges we talked about earlier; and may be subject to early withdrawal charges imposed by the issuing firm. A fixed annuity is just an annuity contract that guarantees a fixed interest rate for a specific number of years—and the money is not invested in the stock market. It's a very conservative way to "park" some of the assets you take out of the stock market until you need them for income.

Alternatively, you could buy a portfolio of individual bonds with maturities greater than four years and use them to create an Income Ladder that will start kicking out income in the fifth year. Or, you could stash the money in a CD or money market mutual fund and hold it there until it's time to buy another SPIA or create another Income Ladder with bonds. There are many different ways to do it and a variety of products that can be used. If you consider using a money market account, keep in mind that they are not insured or guaranteed by the U.S. Government and there is no assurance that they will be able to maintain a stable net asset

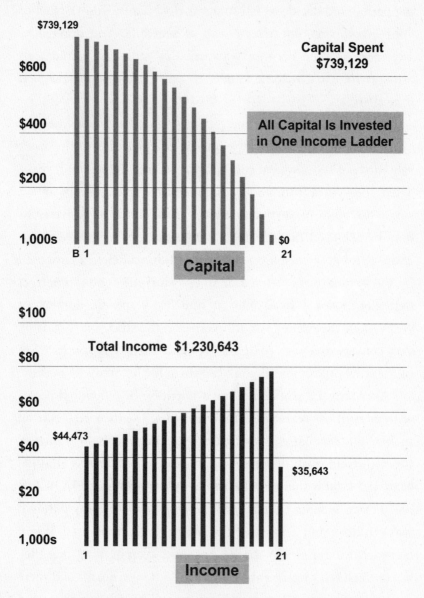

Illustration 34: 30-Year Retirement Portfolio
Capital and Income Values
Conservative Strategy (100% Fixed Income)
(5% Income Ladder Return—Maintain Income)

$739,129

$600

**Capital Spent
$739,129**

$400

**All Capital Is Invested
in One Income Ladder**

$200

1,000s

$0

B 1   21

Capital

$100

Total Income $1,230,643

$80

$60

$44,473

$40

$35,643

$20

1,000s

1   21

Income

For illustration purposes only. Not representative of an actual investment.
Past performance is not a guarantee of future results.

value of $1.00 per share. Money market shares are redeemable at net asset value, which may be more or less than original cost, and their yields fluctuate in the market.

It's Difficult to Maintain the Income Without Stocks

Illustration 34 shows what happens when you invest very conservatively during retirement and decide not to own any stock market investments at all. This example assumes that you follow what may be one of the oldest rules of thumb in the business and decide to get overly conservative with your investments right off the bat.

Since you won't have any stock market investments in your portfolio we can look at the whole process by using just the capital and income graphs. In this example, we assume that your entire capital is put into fixed-income investments earning 5 percent interest and that you take out the same $44,473 per year of inflation-adjusted income. The question is, how long will your money last if you don't own any stocks?

It's important to illustrate the consequences of investing too conservatively because it's one of the two basic tendencies people have. We already talked about the pitfalls of investing too aggressively. Now you will be able to see the consequences of investing too conservatively.

Investing Too Conservatively

By putting all of your money into fixed-income investments and taking out $44,473 of inflation-adjusted income every year, you will completely exhaust the portfolio sometime in year twenty-one. In other words, if you try to maintain the same lifestyle that you were able to get in the illustration reflecting the Grangaard Strategy™, but attempt to do so without owning any stock market investments, your retirement assets will last for only about twenty years.

Over that twenty-year period you will be able to maintain your income, but in year twenty-one you will get just a portion of it, and beyond that you will get nothing at all. If you invest this way, you will only get about $1,230,643 of total income before completely running out of money, compared to $2,115,821, or 72 percent more, using the hypothetical Grangaard Strategy™—which also didn't even touch your capital!

Obviously, if you want to invest this conservatively in retirement you have to be willing to cut your lifestyle expectations significantly. If you don't get the growth you need in the stock market you simply will not be able to earn enough money to sustain a higher lifestyle and you will be forced to plan for less.

Illustration 35: 30-Year Retirement Portfolio
Capital and Income Values
Conservative Strategy (100% Fixed Income)
(5% Income Ladder Return—30-Year Income

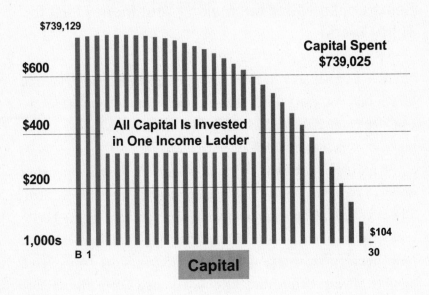

$739,129

**Capital Spent
$739,025**

$600

$400

**All Capital Is Invested
in One Income Ladder**

$200

1,000s

$104

B 1

30

Capital

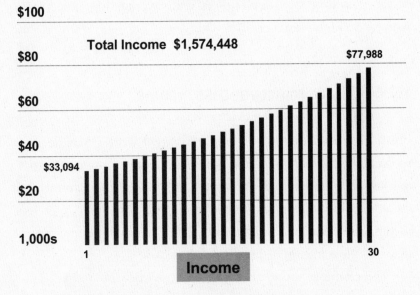

$100

Total Income $1,574,448

$80

$77,988

$60

$40

$33,094

$20

1,000s

1

30

Income

For illustration purposes only. Not representative of an actual investment.
Past performance is not a guarantee of future results.

Being Conservative but Making Your Money Last for Thirty Years

There is another way to think about it. You can also figure out how much you can afford to spend each year if you want to be completely invested in fixed-income investments but want to make your money last at least thirty years.

It may seem strange to think about spending your assets down to zero, but this is the way many retirement plans are actually calculated. You start with whatever you have at the beginning of retirement, assume a fixed rate of return, and calculate how much you can take out of your accounts over some fixed number of years before running out of money. Often, the number of years used in the calculation is your average life expectancy, which you know is generally a bad idea.

You Will Have to Accept Less Income

Illustration 35 shows how a portfolio might work if you decided to do it this way. Again, since you don't plan to own any stock market investments we only need to look at the capital and income graphs. You know you're probably going to get less income each year by investing completely in fixed-income securities, but the question is, how much less?

The example shows that you will only be able to get about $33,094 per year of inflation-protected purchasing power for thirty years, compared to $44,473 using the Grangaard Strategy™ as shown in Illustration 31. In other words, you can get about 34 percent more income with the Grangaard Strategy™ than you can if you put all of your money into fixed-income investments, earn 5 percent per year, and spend it down to zero in thirty years. That's a big difference. And remember, a 100 percent fixed-income portfolio is supposed to give you more comfort in retirement, not less, because it's supposed to be so much safer.

And You Are Flat Broke at the End

In this example you also completely exhaust your retirement capital after thirty years. So instead of increasing the value of your portfolio you actually spend it down to nothing, while at the same time reducing your annual income. These are the kinds of consequences you may face by having a "safer" investment portfolio during retirement. Most people simply cannot afford to do it this way.

The Risk of Investing Too Conservatively During Retirement

The previous two examples demonstrate the potential consequences of not owning stock market investments during retirement. Unless you can afford to live on less income during retirement, and unless you are willing to take a substantial risk that you will outlive your retirement assets, I believe the Grangaard Strategy™ may be the less risky alternative—at least in terms of reducing the risk of not having the lifestyle you want in retirement. It may seem a little riskier to own both stocks and fixed-income investments, but you know that you can use holding periods, diversification, Income Ladders, and thoughtful stock market sales strategies to manage those risks very effectively.

The fact is, with inflation and longer life expectancies, unless you have a lot of extra money, you probably can't afford to be too conservative with your retirement investments. If you are willing to give up the income, it's no problem—but you may not be satisfied with the lifestyle you can achieve with an overly conservative portfolio.

You Have to Figure Out the Right Approach in Your Own Life

The thing to remember about these examples is that they represent only a few of the possible alternatives. You may want to use different rates of return, different holding periods, and different portfolio allocations. You'll probably want to try different inflation rates, consider investing in different segments of the stock market, use different Income Ladder investments, and evaluate different stock market sales strategies. The possibilities are endless—but it's not that difficult to find the right set of assumptions that make the most sense in your own life. You just have to spend a little time getting acquainted with the concepts and ideas in this book and then find a financial professional who can help you figure out what it all means in your own circumstances.

Finding Financial Professionals Who Can Help You Get It Right

You need to create reasonable plans around reasonable estimates and then manage your money properly for the rest of your life. Ultimately, the best way to fine-tune all of the variables around your own unique circumstances is to work with a financial professional who is knowledgeable in these methods and who has the tools required to help you manage your money the right way. We have created a directory on our website that includes a geographical listing of financial advisors that we have taken through a basic level of education in the Grangaard Strategy™. Advisors on the list have attended a training program and acquired the software tools they need to implement the Grangaard Strategy™ as it applies to individual situations. There is more information about our website in the Appendix.

13

Start Working on Your Plan

As a first step in applying the Grangaard Strategy™ in your own life we are going to work through a set of easy-to-use worksheets and look-up tables. After going through the examples you should be able to do some pretty good calculations about your own circumstances and be able to play around with a variety of different planning scenarios.

We obviously can't look at every possible alternative because the tools required to do that can't be distilled into a few simple worksheets, but we can address some of the most pressing questions and use the process to broaden your understanding of how to implement the strategies we've been talking about. With the worksheets you will be able to get a feel for how much money you will need to retire the way you want to and a sense for how much income you will be able to get from the assets you already have.

How Much Money Do You Need to Get the Income You Want?

One of the things most people want to figure out is how much capital they need at retirement to get the income they want for the rest of their lives. This is a fairly typical question for people who still have a few years to get prepared. To answer it, you have to start by deciding how much income you need and then work backward to determine how much capital will be required to provide it.

How Much Income Can You Get from the Assets You Already Have?

The other thing most people want to know when they get close to retirement is how much income they can get from the assets they already have. This becomes an even more important issue as you get closer to retirement since you have less and less time to accumulate additional assets.

Starting Out with the Right Overall Strategy

To figure out how much income you can get from the assets you already have, and to figure out how much capital is required to get the income you want, you have to start by deciding how you will manage your money during retirement in the first place. Until you make this decision you can't even begin to answer these questions. There are many ways to manage a portfolio during retirement—and as we have seen, some of them may be better than others. In the examples that follow we assume that you will be using the Grangaard Strategy™ to manage your assets. In fact, all of the worksheets and look-up tables provided are designed to help you analyze various ways of implementing that strategy.

Other Important Considerations in Retirement Planning

There are certainly other issues you may want to consider. For example, you may want to determine the best investment allocation for your portfolio or be interested in figuring out how to maximize the amount of money you have left at the end of your life for estate and wealth transfer purposes. You might also want to experiment with different inflation rates and different stock market sales strategies. We could go on and on. There are as many financial questions to ask about retirement planning as there are people in retirement. Unfortunately, we can't address all of them with a few simple worksheets and look-up tables. Your financial advisors should be able to help you consider these other issues and tailor a plan to your own circumstances.

General Parameters

To show you how to analyze your own accumulation needs, and to illustrate how to figure out the amount of income you can get from the assets you already have, you need to establish some general parameters and key assumptions. Remember, a lot of variables go into developing a good financial plan—so let's take a quick look at some of the most important ones. In the examples that follow, we make these assumptions:

First, we always assume that you are managing your money inside of tax-deferred accounts—such as annuities, IRAs, or retirement plans. Many people have taxable accounts as well, and although you will probably manage them in much the same way, the outcomes will be different. All of the tables and factors provided in this chapter are relevant only for assets that are protected against both annual income taxes and periodic "liquidity taxes."

Second, we assume that you want to provide quarterly "paychecks" and that you plan to live at least thirty years in retirement.

Third, we assume a 3 percent inflation rate during retirement and a 5 percent average interest rate on your Income Ladder investments.

Fourth, we assume that you put half of your money into Income Ladders and half of it into the stock market.

Fifth, we assume that the money you put into the stock market is split equally between large company stocks and small company stocks and then invested in diversified portfolios of mutual funds within each category.

Sixth, we assume an 8 percent rate of return on large company stocks and a 10 percent rate of return on small company stocks.

And finally, we assume that you use ten-year holding periods for large company stocks and twelve-year holding periods for small company stocks.

Flexible Assumptions

The look-up tables we provide allow you to use many different values for these variables. Since we provide blank worksheets for you to use in creating your own plan, this flexibility will make it possible for you to analyze many alternative planning strategies.

For example, you will be able to use different rate of return assumptions for your stock market investments and different length holding periods for each kind of stock. You will also be able to allocate your portfolios differently between Income Ladder investments and stock market investments.

In fact, we provide three different look-up tables relating to three different asset allocation strategies. The first alternative assumes that you allocate your portfolio equally between Income Ladders and stock market investments. The second alternative assumes that you allocate your investments 30 percent to Income Ladders and 70 percent to stocks, making it a much more aggressive overall allocation. The third alternative assumes that you allocate your investments 70 percent to Income Ladders and 30 percent to stocks, making it by far the most conservative of the three portfolios.

Obviously, these are only three of an unlimited number of potential allocations you might want to consider. We are only scratching the surface of the alternatives that you and a qualified financial professional can work through together.

Pretax Income Needs

One other thing to keep in mind with these examples is that they consider all of your income needs on a pretax basis. As you know, when you invest in tax-deferred accounts you generally only pay income taxes when you take money out of your Income Ladders. We assume it works this way in all of the examples. In other words, you plan in terms of how much money you can take out of your Income Ladders before paying income taxes. Again, getting any more sophisticated in the income tax area demands the skill and experience of a qualified professional.

Calculating How Much Capital You Need to Be Able to Get the Income You Want

Illustration 36, Retirement *Accumulation* Calculator, shows how to figure out how much capital you need to accumulate to get the income you want in retirement. We will work through it in detail to help you understand the process and show you how to use the blank worksheets and look-up tables to create your own plan and take your own needs and circumstances into account.

The first question you have to ask yourself is, what kind of lifestyle do you want in retirement? You can't figure out how much you need to accumulate for retirement if you don't know how much you want to spend during retirement. To answer this question, you have to think back to Chapter 3: Plan for the "Right Amount" of Income to recall the difference between purchasing power and inflation-adjusted income. When you do your retirement planning it's usually easier to think about your lifestyle in terms of current purchasing power, and then convert it into inflation-adjusted income. That's exactly what we are going to do in this example. We will determine how much income you need as if you were going to retire today, and then adjust it to reflect how much more inflation-adjusted income you will need in the future.

Illustration 36: Retirement Accumulation Calculator

Desired Retirement Income in Today's Dollars $___**40,000**___ (1)

Years Until Retirement ___**4**___

Estimated Inflation Rate ___**3**___ %

Inflation Factor from **Inflation Table** ___**1.13**___ (2)

Est. Annual Retirement Income Need – Yr. 1 $___**45,200**___ (3)
(Hypothetical)
                                                (1) X (2)

Factor **B** from **Personal Calculator Table** (#__**1**__) ___**2.36**___ (4)

Est. Annual Retirement Income Need – Yr. 30 $___**106,672**___
(Hypothetical)
                                              (3) X (4)

Factor **C** from **Personal Calculator Table** (#__**1**__) ___**19.65**___ (5)

Retirement Accumulation Needed $___**888,180**___ (6)
(Hypothetical)
                                      (3) X (5)

Factor **D** from **Personal Calculator Table** (#__**1**__) ___**.767**___ (7)

Investment Value in 30 Years in Year 1 Dollars $___**681,234**___
(Hypothetical)
                                            (6) X (7)

Factor **E** from **Personal Calculator Table** (#__**1**__) ___**1.861**___ (8)
(Hypothetical)

Investment Value in 30 Years in Future Dollars $___**1,652,903**___
                                            (6) X (8)

Deciding on Your Lifestyle

In the example in Illustration 36, you see in line (1) that we assume you want $40,000 in today's purchasing power throughout retirement. Of course, when you do your own worksheets you can use any amount you want. The next line shows that you are planning to retire in four years. So you need to decide what rate of inflation to apply to your initial $40,000 lifestyle to convert it into the amount of income you'll need in the first year of retirement, four years from now. Notice in the next line that we assume an inflation rate of 3 percent.

Using the Inflation Table to Determine Your Inflation Factor

Illustration 37 is an Inflation Table. It allows you to use the "Years Until Retirement" and the "Estimated Inflation Rate" from the worksheet to determine an inflation factor that you can use to adjust your retirement income. You simply locate the row for the number of years until retirement—which is four years in this example, and then find the column relating to a 3 percent inflation rate. Running your finger down to the row for four years, and across to the column for 3 percent inflation, you locate the shaded box where the two intersect. There you find a factor of 1.13, which you can now use in the worksheet.

Turning back to Illustration 36, you see that the 1.13 infla-

Illustration 37: Inflation Table

Yrs.	Estimated Inflation Rate							
	1%	2%	3%	4%	5%	6%	7%	8%
1	1.01	1.02	1.03	1.04	1.05	1.06	1.07	1.08
2	1.02	1.04	1.06	1.08	1.10	1.12	1.14	1.17
3	1.03	1.06	1.09	1.12	1.16	1.19	1.23	1.26
4	1.04	1.08	1.13	1.17	1.22	1.26	1.31	1.36
5	1.05	1.10	1.16	1.22	1.28	1.34	1.40	1.47
6	1.06	1.13	1.19	1.27	1.34	1.42	1.50	1.59
7	1.07	1.15	1.23	1.32	1.41	1.50	1.61	1.71
8	1.08	1.17	1.27	1.37	1.48	1.59	1.72	1.85
9	1.09	1.20	1.30	1.42	1.55	1.69	1.84	2.00
10	1.10	1.22	1.34	1.48	1.63	1.79	1.97	2.16
11	1.12	1.24	1.38	1.54	1.71	1.90	2.10	2.33
12	1.13	1.27	1.43	1.60	1.80	2.01	2.25	2.52
13	1.14	1.29	1.47	1.67	1.89	2.13	2.41	2.72
14	1.15	1.32	1.51	1.73	1.98	2.26	2.58	2.94
15	1.16	1.35	1.56	1.80	2.08	2.40	2.76	3.17
16	1.17	1.37	1.60	1.87	2.18	2.54	2.95	3.43
17	1.18	1.40	1.65	1.95	2.29	2.69	3.16	3.70
18	1.20	1.43	1.70	2.03	2.41	2.85	3.38	4.00
19	1.21	1.46	1.75	2.11	2.53	3.03	3.62	4.32
20	1.22	1.49	1.81	2.19	2.65	3.21	3.87	4.66

tion factor has been pulled forward to line (2) in the worksheet. Then you simply multiply the $40,000 lifestyle in line (1) by the inflation factor of 1.13 in line (2) to determine an estimated income need for the first year of retirement—$45,200 as shown in the first shaded box in line (3). It's that easy. You now know how much income you will need in the first year of retirement to provide the same lifestyle that $40,000 will provide today.

Income Needed in the Last Year of Retirement

The next step is to calculate how much you will need in the last year of retirement. This will give you a better feel for how much income you will need to provide overall, and how much it will have to increase over this thirty-year retirement period. To determine this amount you have to get the next calculation factor from Illustration 38, Personal Calculator Table #1.

Using the Personal Calculator Tables

Let's spend a couple minutes exploring Personal Calculator Table #1 (PCT #1). Once you understand how it works you will also be able to use Personal Calculator Tables #2 and #3—because they work exactly the same way. Notice that PCT #1 allocates 50 percent of your assets to Income Ladder investments and 50 percent to stock market investments, split equally between large company stocks and small company stocks.

Illustration 38: Personal Calculator Table #1
Income Ladder Allocation 50%
Large Company Stock Allocation 25%
Small Company Stock Allocation 25%

Income Ladder Return 5%	Large Company Stocks			
	5-Year Holding Period		10-Year Holding Period	
	8% Return	10% Return	8% Return	10% Return
Small Company Stocks — 6-Year Holding Period — 10% Return	A .050 B 2.36 C 19.96 D .665 E 1.614	A .055 B 2.36 C 18.21 D .699 E 1.697	A .049 B 2.36 C 20.24 D .718 E 1.742	A .055 B 2.36 C 18.35 D .789 E 1.915
Small Company Stocks — 6-Year Holding Period — 12% Return	A .056 B 2.36 C 17.92 D .706 E 1.713	A .061 B 2.36 C 16.47 D .736 E 1.786	A .055 B 2.36 C 18.15 D .758 E 1.841	A .060 B 2.36 C 16.64 D .834 E 2.023
Small Company Stocks — 12-Year Holding Period — 10% Return	A .050 B 2.36 C 19.80 D .759 E 1.842	A .055 B 2.36 C 18.05 D .789 E 1.915	A .051 B 2.36 C 19.65 D .767 E 1.861	A .057 B 2.36 C 17.61 D .805 E 1.954
Small Company Stocks — 12-Year Holding Period — 12% Return	A .056 B 2.36 C 17.86 D .917 E 2.227	A .061 B 2.36 C 16.42 D .947 E 2.300	A .057 B 2.36 C 17.70 D .921 E 2.236	A .060 B 2.36 C 16.56 D 1.041 E 2.527

For illustration purposes only. Not representative of an actual investment.
Higher volatility has historically been associated with higher rates of return,
and average returns have had a tendency to fluctuate from year to year.

Illustration 39: Personal Calculator Table #2
Income Ladder Allocation 30%
Large Company Stock Allocation 35%
Small Company Stock Allocation 35%

Income Ladder Return 5%			Large Company Stocks			
			5-Year Holding Period		10-Year Holding Period	
			8% Return	10% Return	8% Return	10% Return
Small Company Stocks	6-Year Holding Period	10% Return	A .052 B 2.36 C 19.12 D .093 E 2.253	A .059 B 2.36 C 16.89 D .097 E 2.351	A .051 B 2.36 C 19.46 D .999 E 2.421	A .057 B 2.36 C 17.61 D 1.212 E 2.941
		12% Return	A .060 B 2.36 C 16.61 D .099 E 2.399	A .067 B 2.36 C 14.90 D 1.029 E 2.497	A .059 B 2.36 C 16.86 D 1.059 E 2.570	A .060 B 2.36 C 16.64 D 1.726 E 4.182
	12-Year Holding Period	10% Return	A .044 B 2.36 C 22.57 D 1.682 E 4.084	A .050 B 2.36 C 24.94 D 1.823 E 4.424	A .040 B 2.36 C 24.94 D 2.028 E 4.922	A .040 B 2.36 C 24.94 D 2.660 E 6.456
		12% Return	A .044 B 2.36 C 22.57 D 3.064 E 7.437	A .050 B 2.36 C 20.04 D 3.226 E 7.830	A .040 B 2.36 C 24.94 D 3.503 E 8.503	A .040 B 2.36 C 24.94 D 4.291 E 10.416

For illustration purposes only. Not representative of an actual investment.
Higher volatility has historically been associated with higher rates of return,
and average returns have had a tendency to fluctuate from year to year.

Illustration 40: Personal Calculator Table #3
Income Ladder Allocation 70%
Large Company Stock Allocation 15%
Small Company Stock Allocation 15%

Income Ladder Return 5%			Large Company Stocks			
			5-Year Holding Period		10-Year Holding Period	
			8% Return	10% Return	8% Return	10% Return
Small Company Stocks	6-Year Holding Period	10% Return	A .048 B 2.36 C 20.88 D .402 E .976	A .051 B 2.36 C 19.65 D .418 E 1.014	A .048 B 2.36 C 21.01 D .429 E 1.041	A .051 B 2.36 C 19.76 D .474 E 1.150
		12% Return	A .051 B 2.36 C 19.46 D .423 E 1.027	A .054 B 2.36 C 18.42 D .443 E 1.075	A .051 B 2.36 C 19.65 D .458 E 1.112	A .054 B 2.36 C 18.55 D .503 E 1.221
	12-Year Holding Period	10% Return	A .050 B 2.36 C 20.16 D .399 E .968	A .053 B 2.36 C 19.05 D .418 E 1.016	A .049 B 2.36 C 20.33 D .430 E 1.043	A .052 B 2.36 C 19.16 D .475 E 1.152
		12% Return	A .055 B 2.36 C 18.32 D .424 E 1.030	A .058 B 2.36 C 17.39 D .444 E 1.078	A .054 B 2.36 C 18.45 D .455 E 1.105	A .057 B 2.36 C 17.48 D .500 E 1.214

For illustration purposes only. Not representative of an actual investment.
Higher volatility has historically been associated with higher rates of return,
and average returns have had a tendency to fluctuate from year to year.

Different Portfolio Allocations

Personal Calculator Table #2 relates to a much more aggressive overall portfolio allocation of 30 percent to Income Ladder investments and 70 percent to stock market investments, while Personal Calculator Table #3 represents a more conservative investment strategy with an allocation of 70 percent to Income Ladders and 30 percent to equities. The three Personal Calculator Tables will allow you to assess a variety of different asset allocation strategies in your own life.

A Guided Tour of the Personal Calculator Table

Before we get back to the worksheet we need to take a quick tour through PCT #1 to see how it works. First, large company stocks are shown across the top, with an option to use either five-year or ten-year holding periods and either 8 percent or 10 percent rates of return. Then, small company stocks are shown along the left side, with an option to use either six- or twelve-year holding periods and 10 or 12 percent rates of return.

Overall, this gives you a large number of possible combinations of holding periods and rates of return within a portfolio allocated fifty-fifty between stocks and fixed-income investments. For this example we use the factors highlighted in the shaded box relating to ten-year holding periods and 8 percent rates of return for large company stocks and twelve-year holding periods and 10 percent rates of return for small company stocks. Income Ladder investments are expected to earn a 5 percent average rate of interest. To use any of the Personal Calculator Tables you simply determine which of the three initial portfolio allocations to use, select the appropriate table, then decide on rates of return and holding periods for each segment of the stock market. The tables then provide a set of factors you can use to complete the worksheets.

Completing the Accumulation Example

Let's get back to Illustration 36 to see how much money you would need to accumulate for retirement. So far, we have completed the analysis through line (3)—the amount of income you need in the first year of retirement—or $45,200. But we also want to know how much income you will need thirty years from now if inflation averages 3 percent per year.

To figure it out, simply go to the shaded box in PCT #1 and select Factor B in the table—which is 2.36. Then, pull it forward to line (4) in the worksheet and multiply it by the $45,200 in line (3) to determine the amount of income your portfolio will need to provide in the thirtieth year of retirement. The Estimated Annual Retirement Income Need in Year 30 is $106,672, which should be enough to maintain the purchasing power of $45,200 at a 3 percent inflation rate for thirty years. (Note that we have referenced PCT #1 in the worksheet. Since the rest of the factors in this example also come from the same table, you will see that a "1" has been indicated throughout.)

While we're at it, let's gather up all the rest of the factors we'll need from PCT #1 to complete the worksheet. Factor C, or 19.65, pulls forward to line (5); Factor D, or .767 pulls forward to line (7); and Factor E, or 1.861, pulls forward to line (8).

How Much Do You Need to Accumulate?

The whole point of this exercise is to determine how much money you need to accumulate to provide the income you want throughout retirement. So the next step is to multiply Factor C, or 19.65, by the $45,200 of purchasing power needed each year in line (3) to determine the total accumulation amount required. Notice in the third shaded box that you need to accumulate about $888,180 to be able to generate the increasing amounts of income you desire. That's the amount of money you need in a tax-deferred investment account to be able to generate the required amounts of pretax income for thirty years.

How Much Will You Have Left at the End of Retirement?

One of the other things people often want to know is how much money they will have left at the end of their life. We've talked about the likelihood that if you manage your money the right way during retirement you might end up with quite a bit. That's why I said earlier that when you finish your retirement planning you will probably need to move on to your estate and wealth transfer planning. To complete the example, let's determine how much will be left at the end of thirty years.

To do this you simply multiply Factor D, or .767, by the $888,180 in line (6) to arrive at $681,234. That's the anticipated value of your account at the end of thirty years—in terms of the purchasing power you had on the first day of retirement. So in this example you will have used up about $206,946 of value, or about 23 percent of the beginning portfolio—which probably isn't much of a concern given the fact that you still have plenty left if you live even longer.

Ending Value in Inflation-Adjusted Dollars

We also want to know how much inflation-adjusted capital we will have left at the end of thirty years, since that's the amount you will need to consider for estate tax and wealth transfer purposes. To calculate that amount, you simply multiply Factor E, or 1.861, by your initial retirement accumulation of $888,180 to arrive at an ending inflation-adjusted dollar amount of $1,652,903. That's the amount of money you can expect to have at the end of thirty years. Obviously, you will want to plan for the appropriate distribution of those assets.

Using the Worksheets and Look-Up Tables

That's how simple it is to figure out how much money you need to accumulate to get the lifestyle you want in retirement. It's easy to use the worksheets and look-up tables to figure out how much you need to accumulate for any given set of variables. Now that you know how to use them, you can analyze many different scenarios for yourself. Simply use the blank worksheet in Illustration 41 and the look-up tables in Illustrations 37, 38, 39, and 40 to evaluate a wide variety of possibilities.

Changing any of the assumptions—such as holding periods, rates of return, investment allocation percentages, inflation rates, income needs, or any of the other factors will change the outcome. If you spend a few minutes with the worksheets and look-up tables you will be able to evaluate what those changes will be for many different portfolios. If you analyze a few different scenarios for yourself you will start to get a better feel for your own circumstances. The worksheets and tables won't allow you to fine-tune your plan as much as you may want to, and they won't allow you to look at all of the potential investment scenarios you might want to consider, but they will get you off on the right foot. Ultimately, they should prepare you to have much better conversations with your advisors when you start talking to them about using these strategies to manage your own money during retirement.

Illustration 41: Retirement Accumulation Calculator

Desired Retirement Income in Today's Dollars $______________ **(1)**

Years Until Retirement __________

Estimated Inflation Rate __________%

Inflation Factor from **Inflation Table** __________ **(2)**

Est. Annual Retirement Income Need—Yr. 1 $______________ **(3)**
(Hypothetical) (1) X (2)

Factor B from **Personal Calculator Table (#____)** __________ **(4)**

Est. Annual Retirement Income Need—Yr. 30 $______________
(Hypothetical) (3) X (4)

Factor C from **Personal Calculator Table (#____)** __________ **(5)**

Retirement Accumulation Needed $______________ **(6)**
(Hypothetical) (3) X (5)

Factor D from **Personal Calculator Table (#____)** __________ **(7)**

Investment Value in 30 Years in Year 1 Dollars $______________
(Hypothetical) (6) X (7)

Factor E from **Personal Calculator Table (#____)** __________ **(8)**

Investment Value in 30 Years in Future Dollars $______________
(Hypothetical) (6) X (8)

For illustration purposes only. Not representative of an actual investment. An individual investor's results may vary. All assumptions and computational results are hypothetical in nature. There are no guarentees that you will achieve the results shown. You should consult with a financial professional.

Calculating How Much Income You Can Get from the Assets You Already Have

As I mentioned earlier, the other big issue most people want to address is how much income they can get from the retirement assets they already have. The Retirement *Accumulation* Calculator worksheet we just completed was used to figure out how much capital you need to provide the amount of income you want in retirement. This is a common type of analysis for people who still have a few years to prepare, or for others who are trying to figure out if a gap still exists between their expectations and their ability to meet them. However, Illustration 42, Retirement *Income* Calculator, assumes that you have already accumulated your retirement assets and therefore need to figure out how much income you can get from the capital you already have. This is particularly important for people already in retirement or who are getting close, and who need to get a feel for the capacity of their resources to generate income for the rest of their life.

Using the Retirement *Income* Calculator Worksheets

Illustration 42 also uses PCT #1 for many of the calculation factors you need to do the analysis. However, the Retirement *Income* Calculator worksheet is a little different than the Retirement *Accumulation* Calculator worksheet in that you start the

Illustration 42: Retirement Income Calculator

Current Investment Value in Today's Dollars $ **475,000** **(1)**

Years Until Retirement **4**

Estimated Investment Rate of Return **7** %

Investment Factor from **Investment Table** **1.31** **(2)**

Estimated Investment Value at Retirement $ **622,250** **(3)**
(Hypothetical) (1) X (2)

Factor **A** from **Personal Calculator Table (# 1)** **.051** **(4)**

Est. Annual Retirement Income—Yr. 1 $ **31,735** **(5)**
(Hypothetical) (3) X (4)

Factor **B** from **Personal Calculator Table (# 1)** **2.36** **(6)**

Est. Annual Retirement Income—Yr. 30 $ **74,895**
(Hypothetical) (5) X (6)

Factor **D** from **Personal Calculator Table (# 1)** **.767** **(7)**

Investment Value in 30 Years in Year 1 Dollars $ **477,266**
(Hypothetical) (3) X (7)

Factor **E** from **Personal Calculator Table (# 1)** **1.861** **(8)**

Investment Value in 30 Years in Future Dollars $ **1,158,007**
(Hypothetical) (3) X (8)

For illustration purposes only. Not representative of an actual investment. An individual investor's results may vary. All assumptions and computational results are hypothetical in nature. There are no guarentees that you will achieve the results shown. You should consult with a financial professional.

analysis by determining how much capital you already have, rather than how much income you want.

You start with the current value of your investments—which in this example is $475,000. Then, just like in the accumulation example, you assume that you will retire in four years. The next question, however, is a little different. Rather than selecting an expected inflation rate to adjust your income need, you instead select a rate of return that you expect to earn on your investments over the next four years.

Obviously, the $475,000 you already have should continue to grow at some rate of return until you retire. You need to decide what that rate of return will be in order to determine what the $475,000 will be worth at the beginning of retirement. As always, you need to consider the long-term historical average annual rates of return for the markets you are investing in when making this decision. In the example, we assume that your assets will grow at 7 percent per year during the four years prior to retirement.

Using the Investment Table to Get an Investment Factor

The Investment Table in Illustration 43 allows us to determine an investment factor. For our purposes, simply go down the left-hand column to the row for four years, across the upper row to the column for 7 percent, and find the box where the two intersect. The investment factor, shaded in gray, is 1.31. Then, you

Illustration 43: Investment Table

Yrs.	Estimated Investment Growth Rate							
	5%	6%	7%	8%	9%	10%	11%	12%
1	1.05	1.06	1.07	1.08	1.09	1.10	1.11	1.12
2	1.10	1.12	1.14	1.17	1.19	1.21	1.23	1.25
3	1.16	1.19	1.23	1.26	1.30	1.33	1.37	1.40
4	1.22	1.26	1.31	1.36	1.41	1.46	1.52	1.57
5	1.28	1.34	1.40	1.47	1.54	1.61	1.69	1.76
6	1.34	1.42	1.50	1.59	1.68	1.77	1.87	1.97
7	1.41	1.50	1.61	1.71	1.83	1.95	2.08	2.21
8	1.48	1.59	1.72	1.85	1.99	2.14	2.30	2.48
9	1.55	1.69	1.84	2.00	2.17	2.36	2.56	2.77
10	1.63	1.79	1.97	2.16	2.37	2.59	2.84	3.11
11	1.71	1.90	2.10	2.33	2.58	2.85	3.15	3.48
12	1.80	2.01	2.25	2.52	2.81	3.14	3.50	3.90
13	1.89	2.13	2.41	2.72	3.07	3.45	3.88	4.36
14	1.98	2.26	2.58	2.94	3.34	3.80	4.31	4.89
15	2.08	2.40	2.76	3.17	3.64	4.18	4.78	5.47
16	2.18	2.54	2.95	3.43	3.97	4.59	5.31	6.13
17	2.29	2.69	3.16	3.70	4.33	5.05	5.90	6.87
18	2.41	2.85	3.38	4.00	4.72	5.56	6.54	7.69
19	2.53	3.03	3.62	4.32	5.14	6.12	7.26	8.61
20	2.65	3.21	3.87	4.66	5.60	6.73	8.06	9.65

simply pull that factor forward to line (2) in the worksheet and multiply it by the beginning investment value of $475,000 in line (1) to arrive at an estimated investment value of $622,250 as of the beginning of retirement, shown in the first shaded box in line (3). That's the amount of money you can expect to have at the beginning of retirement four years from now.

How Much Income Can You Get?

Of course the reason you are using this worksheet in the first place is to figure out how much income you can get from that $622,250 if you manage it properly during retirement. To do that, you go back to the highlighted section of PCT #1 and pull all the necessary calculation factors forward to the worksheet. Factor A, or .051, goes to line (4); Factor B, or 2.36, goes to line (6); Factor D, or .767 goes to line (7); and Factor E, or 1.861, goes to line (8).

Then, to figure out how much inflation-adjusted income you should be able to get out of the portfolio over the next thirty years you simply multiply the .051 factor in line (4) by the total capital amount of $622,250 in line (3). The answer, shown in line (5), is $31,735. That's how much inflation-adjusted income you should be able to generate throughout retirement. Of course you always want to know how much income will be needed in year thirty to maintain that $31,735 of purchasing power. So you multiply the 2.36 factor in line (6) by the $31,735 in line (5) to determine that the portfolio will provide $74,895 of income in the thirtieth year of retirement, just to maintain the purchasing power of the initial $31,735.

How Much Do You Have Left?

To determine how much you are likely to have left at the end of your life, you simply multiply Factor D, or .767 by your beginning portfolio value of $622,250 in line (3), to get an ending portfolio value of $477,266 as shown in the fourth gray box. Then, you multiply Factor E, or 1.861, in line (8), by the same $622,250 beginning account value in line (3) to determine the ending portfolio amount in inflation-adjusted dollars—which is $1,158,007, as shown in the last shaded box.

So you should be able to get about $31,735 of inflation-protected income for thirty years, starting with $622,250 in capital, and will experience about a 23 percent reduction in assets—or in this case, a drop of about $144,984 in value. And of course, for estate planning purposes, you will probably have a significant amount of money to deal with.

There Are a Lot of Scenarios

We've discussed the variables and worked through two common examples. Illustration 36 relates to how much you need to accumulate for retirement, and Illustration 42 concerns how much income you can get from the assets you already have. These examples should give you a much better feel for the consequences of using the Grangaard Strategy™. But remember, there are literally thousands of ways to pull it all together, and each of them leads to significantly different outcomes. That's why it's so important to use the blank worksheets to evaluate a variety of different scenarios and to work with financial professionals who have the tools required to help you deal with all of the other alternatives. Blank Illustration 41 will help you analyze different accumulation scenarios, and blank Illustration 44 will help you analyze different income scenarios. Clearly, manual worksheets like these only allow you to look at a few of the possibilities—which is a great way to get started but not the best way to finish.

Using the Worksheets and Getting Help

Play around with the examples and use the blank worksheets to try some additional scenarios. Ultimately, you should be much better positioned to talk with your advisors about what you're thinking, about what they're thinking, and about how you can work together to create a comprehensive retirement plan. Think about everything we've discussed, get some experience with the worksheets, and call a financial professional. Or, if you are not working with a financial professional, go to our website to find someone who is "trained" in using the Grangaard Strategy™ to manage money during retirement.

It's time to get started. Principle #12 says Take Action Now, because it's never too early and it's never too late to create your

Illustration 44: Retirement Income Calculator

Current Investment Value in Today's Dollars $__________ **(1)**

Years Until Retirement __________

Estimated Investment Rate of Return __________%

Investment Factor from **Investment Table** __________ **(2)**

Estimated Investment Value at Retirement $__________ **(3)**
(Hypothetical) (1) X (2)

Factor **A** from **Personal Calculator Table (#____)** __________ **(4)**

Est. Annual Retirement Income—Yr. 1 $__________ **(5)**
(Hypothetical) (3) X (4)

Factor **B** from **Personal Calculator Table (#____)** __________ **(6)**

Est. Annual Retirement Income—Yr. 30 $__________
(Hypothetical) (5) X (6)

Factor **D** from **Personal Calculator Table (#____)** __________ **(7)**

Investment Value in 30 Years in Year 1 Dollars $__________
(Hypothetical) (3) X (7)

Factor **E** from **Personal Calculator Table (#____)** __________ **(8)**

Investment Value in 30 Years in Future Dollars $__________
(Hypothetical) (3) X (8)

For illustration purposes only. Not representative of an actual investment. An individual investor's results may vary. All assumptions and computational results are hypothetical in nature. There are no guarentees that you will achieve the results shown. You should consult with a financial professional.

financial plan. Remember, most people don't plan to fail, they simply fail to plan. I urge you to get started today. If you have any questions about the Grangaard Strategy™, about choosing a financial professional, or about any of our other products or services, you can find more information in the Appendix.

Get started now—and good luck!

APPENDIX

Selecting a Financial Professional

Keep in mind that there are many kinds of financial professionals and they get paid in many different ways. You need to be extremely cautious in selecting your advisors, because as the old saying goes—"choose your advisor and you have chosen your advice." You need to decide who to work with and how you want to pay them. Some advisors earn commissions, some are paid based upon assets under management, and still others charge a flat hourly rate. There are no right ways and no wrong ways to charge for financial planning services—but there are better and worse ways to manage your money during retirement. Make sure you are comfortable with your advisor; make sure you are comfortable with how they are getting paid; and make sure you are comfortable with their approach to helping you manage your money during retirement. One of the best ways to select an advisor is to talk with your friends and relatives about who they use.

Questions to Ask a Financial Professional

Most financial planning professionals agree that there are a number of questions you should ask a potential advisor. In addition to finding out whether they are familiar with the Grangaard Strategy™ and if they have the tools they need to implement it, you should also go through some of these other questions when interviewing a potential advisor.

What kinds of experience do you have and who are your typical clients?

What are your qualifications, professional designations, licenses, and memberships?

What did you do before you became a financial planner?

How long have you lived here?

What kinds of products and services do you offer?

What is your overall approach to financial planning before retirement?

What is your overall approach to financial planning after retirement?

Are you the only person I will be working with or do you use a team approach?

Can you work with my other advisors and can you make referrals?

How will I pay you for your services and how much do you typically charge?

Have you ever been disciplined for unlawful or unethical acts in your profession?

Have you ever been convicted of a crime?

Do you provide a written agreement and engagement letter?

How long have you been providing financial planning advice?

Resources to Check the Disciplinary History of a Financial Professional

Certified Financial Planner Board of Standards: 888-CFP-MARK

North American Securities Administrators Association: 888-84-NASAA

National Association of Insurance Commissioners: 816-842-3600

National Association of Securities Dealers: 800-289-9999

Securities and Exchange Commission: 800-732-0330

Resources to Help You Find a Financial Professional

Financial Planning Association: 800-647-6340

National Association of Personal Financial Advisors: 888-FEE-ONLY

American Institute of Certified Public Accountants Personal Financial Planning Division: 800-862-4272

American Society of CLU & ChFC: 800-392-6900

Finding a "Trained" Grangaard Strategy™ Advisor

Visit www.thegrangaardstrategy.com for a list of advisors who have attended a Grangaard Strategy™ Training Program

For more information about Financial Education, Inc., and our products and services, or about how you can find a "Trained" Grangaard Strategy™ advisor in your area, contact us at the numbers and address below, or visit one of our websites.

Financial Education, Inc.
1856 Grand Avenue
Saint Paul, MN 55105

TELEPHONE 651-695-0440
FAX 651-695-1171
EMAIL paul@fied.com
WEBSITE For information about Financial Education, Inc. visit us at: www.fied.com

For a list of "trained" Grangaard Strategy™ advisors visit us at: www.thegrangaardstrategy.com

INDEX